BREWING
MEAD

BREWING MEAD

W·A·S·S·A·I·L·!
IN MAZERS OF MEAD

LT. COLONEL ROBERT GAYRE
GAYRE & NIGG
WITH CHARLIE PAPAZIAN

*The Intriguing History
of the
Beverage of Kings
and
Easy, Step-by-Step
Instructions
for Brewing It At Home*

Brewers Publications — Boulder, Colorado

Wassail! In Mazers of Mead
by G. Robert Gayre
Copyright © 1986 by G. Robert Gayre, Gayre & Nigg
First Published in 1948

Brewing Mead
by Charlie Papazian
Copyright © 1986 by Charlie Papazian

ISBN 0-937381-00-4
Printed in the United States of America
10 9 8 7 6

Published by Brewers Publications
A division of the Association of Brewers.
PO Box 1679, Boulder, Colorado 80306-1679 USA
Tel. (303) 447-0816 • FAX (303) 447-2825

Direct all inquiries/orders to the above address.

Cover design by David Bjorkman
and Virginia Thomas, *David Thomas and Associates.*

Lt. Colonel Robert Gayre, M.A., D.Sc.

Site   nú   tó   symle
Sit   now to   banquet

and   onsæl   meodo
and   unseal   with mead

sige   hréther   secgum
brave   breast   with warriors.
(Beowulf being bidden by King
Hrothgar at Hart Hall.)

CONTENTS

ILLUSTRATIONS

ACKNOWLEDGMENTS

I WISH to express my thanks to my friend and colleague, Lt.-Colonel W. H. Sherwood, D.Litt., for his kindness in going through this MS. and making corrections, as a result of which several passages have been made less obscure and more easily understandable. To my friend Mr. C. Harold Ridge, Managing Director of Messrs. Phillimore & Company Limited, I wish to convey my thanks for the trouble he has taken in seeing this book through the press, and for ensuring a standard of production and craftmanship not easily come by in these days of severe shortages of materials and of labour.

This new edition has been brought out through the enthusiastic support of Mr. Charlie Papazian of the American Homebrewers Association, and as a consequence, a final chapter on how to manufacture mead has been added.

FOREWORD

REMEMBERING recently a lunch with a distinguished cleric at which he had provided an excellent bottle of Orvieto, a rare luxury in these days of want, at which we had discussed mead and the drinking habits and vessels of our forebears, I decided to write a short account of these. For they are subjects upon which there is very little written and known to-day and it is perhaps worth while recording what I have been gathering together for some years upon *mead, sack, metheglin, cyser*, and the *pyment* and *clarre* wine of Chaucer.

Owing to the circumstances in which it has been written this small book does not set out to say the last word upon the subject. But it is hoped that it will do something towards an understanding of an obscure study, and throw light upon the development of drinking among our forebears.

The drinking and eating habits of our ancestors are of interest to all who value the culture which they have inherited. With time customs and habits change and old ways are forgotten, and with the passing of centuries much is forgotten which ought to be remembered. A study of old herbals and cookery books provides ample proof of that fact. Change is not always progress—although it is often mistaken for it, and in no subject is that better illustrated than in the one now in hand. Mead did not become a rarity because it was inferior to what took its place. It suffered the effects of many influences, not least among which were economic and social changes, combined with that curious shortness of memory which allows good things to be forgotten so long as there is some ready substitute at hand. But since these changes which struck at the mead-making culture of our forebears there have been changes again and again, as we shall see, and one of the very reasons which helped to drive out mead, the cheapness of foreign wine, for example, no longer exists. On the contrary the economic conditions have been reversed. But man's memory being short, and the art of mead-making being almost forgotten, we do not, as we should otherwise expect, see a recovery of prosperity for one of the finest natural liquors, but an attempt instead to produce synthetic " Vermouths ", " Burgundies ", " Champagnes ", and " Clarets " on our own soil. Here is not progress but retrogression. In this case, to progress we should go back and recapture from the past that which was better than what we have at present. But curiously enough (as we shall see so far as mead is concerned) in this matter of wine-drinking in England and all the furnishings which go with it, we have not progressed since the Middle Ages but very markedly degenerated. In the real art of making and drinking wines, whether from the grape or honey, individualism stands high. You do not value a wine as a " Claret " or a " Burgundy " but as a certain Claret or Burgundy. But modern man who only asks for an approximate combination of flavours which resemble a " Port ", " Sherry ", or a " Claret " without asking from whom or whence it comes, has dropped from the highly individualistic standard to a very low and common one.

In the same way our furnishings of the wine services has declined. It was the habit to have beautifully wrought cups and bowls made separately and at different times as they were required. But nowadays a dozen standard-shaped vessels for each type of wine suffice. The love of being a little different, to have something wrought to one's own taste, is going, and in its stead we have everything to " match " as a dominant, but unfortunate passion of present-day life. With it, in all its manifestations, the art is going out of living, and that individualism, which is so necessary to resist the cramping influences of this machine-minded age, becomes more difficult to maintain.

G. R. G.

THE MEAD HOUSE,
    GULVAL, CORNWALL,
        June, 1948.

INTRODUCTION

FROM the earliest times the feast in the more magnificent form, and the plain cup on the simpler occasion, have been the proper and fitting demonstration of good cheer and fellowship. Only within the last hundred years, or a little more, has that curious phenomenon, " Tee-totalism ", arisen, with all its blighting influence upon the human spirit. At all ages has intemperance been rightly condemned—it is an abuse, like gluttony, of the natural foods and appetites of man. But to say that wine and beer must be banished, because of their abuse, is as insane as to fast unto death because of the dangers of over-eating. Logically, it would seem that smoking, snuff- and drug-taking are more unnatural and more worthy of attack by reformers than the natural drinks which man has drunk throughout all ages.

If the antagonism to drinking is that it produces drunkenness—the answer is education and temperance. No lover of wine, knowing what he is drinking and appreciating it, and knowing all the care bestowed upon it, is so sottish as to become bestial upon this hallmark of the progress of man's civilization. If it is said that drink causes the poor to waste their money, it is granted that drunkenness has always done so, and the corrective to that is already suggested. So far as it is argued that the modern price is so high that it causes privation, the correct answer is a reduction of taxation. Such high prices in the first place were created by " teetotalism " in an effort to make liquor prohibitive to the masses. But it may be argued with some force that tobacco, picture-going and many other modern habits which lack the socially desirable qualities of companionship and fellowship induced by the bowl and the inn, cause a far greater waste of money to the poor.

If it is said that liquor is bad for the health this can be denied vigorously. There are times when it is the very opposite and only the excess of it can be harmful. Further-more, it is often seen how the common man, the soldier or farm labourer, after an evening quietly spent in the " Local ", with other folk, the newspaper and the dart-board, returns to barracks or cottage psychologically fitter than before because of the very uplift produced by the fellowship which has arisen over his pewter tankard.

Indeed, by attempting to ban as houses of ill-repute the Tavern and the Inn the Tee-total movement has done a decided disservice to the social development of England. Its attack on drunkenness, the gin shop and all that sordidness which Dickens so graphically portrays was justified, but its methods were wrong, and like American prohibition they have not resulted in a social benefit. Prohibition being a more extreme doctrine than English tee-totalism has produced more extreme and unfortunate results. There, as here, not only has it failed to ban alcohol, but it has created vicious drinking habits—and the extreme abuse of alcohol and the crude love of raw spirits among Americans, with the destruc-tion of standards of drinking, must in some measure be due to the Prohibition attempt. Psychologically too, the effect of denying the young the use of small ale, and other similar and suitable drinks, means that when the young begin to strike out on their own they start on a life of " pub-crawling " —because it is, to them, a " clever " thing to do—an assertion of their independence to drink this forbidden stuff.

May the day come again, when Englishmen may be wise enough to drink well, and when and where they will, and when an Englishman's table, be he archbishop, scholar or trade unionist, shall always carry the fitting liquor upon it suitable to his tastes and needs. And may that day see the inns places of refreshment and social good feeling, where lawyer or parson—and Nonconformist minister, too—can meet their friends, clients and parishioners as they did of old without loss of caste or need for explanation. To drink well, means also to drink with understanding, and to drink with understanding does not mean to drink wantonly. The lie to that is given by all the old parish churches of England. With our background of prejudice against a rational life it is curious to ponder on these old buildings, examples of devotion, good fellowship and beauty such as few countries possess, and then to remember that those beautiful old churches of East Anglia, for instance, which rise up like cathedrals in the quiet English landscape, were maintained and partly built out of the profits of the " Church Ales " [1] when the whole village gathered around sir parson and in a merry festival they celebrated a church feast, and, as a result, added more stone and mortar, more timber and craftsmanship to the heritage of England. A memorial of such a festival is to be found at Sygate in Norfolk, where there is carved on the gallery of the Church :

> " God speed the plough
> And give us good ale enow . . .
> Be merry and glade,
> With good ale was this work made."

Another at Thorpe-le-Soken, Essex, is commemorated, on the screen, which dates from about 1480, by the information :

> " This cost is the bachelers
> made by ales thesn be
> ther med."

In the Tudor period these Church Ales were usually held on Sundays. A practice which would be considered to-day as shocking as the drinking of ale at a religious festival. The Whitsun feasts in some churches are a survival (without the ale!) of the regular Church Ales.

Besides Church Ales there were Clerk Ales for the benefit of the parson. I should imagine that these were more effective than the Easter collections are to-day in raising his stipend. [2]

To-day I fear that things are sadly changed. I remember during the late war my battery was stationed in a certain village which had an ancient church witnessing to that great civilization of old England. Ours was a strange battery; I was the only interloper in it, a southerner, having been posted to it after our retreat from France. Excepting for their battery captain I think from the major downwards they all came from the same town. If a man misbehaved himself it was sufficient for the battery commander to give it out on parade that if it happened again he would write to his father, and these big rough northern men wilted before this terrible threat. They were singularly like a family. Thus it came about that they all went to church in a body without any more desire to default than there was for what the army calls " crime " in the battery. Our methods of church-going, although very natural, were rather singular in this age. We would march straight out of the village church and up the street, until reaching The Bell, the battery halted and was dismissed. The men poured into the general bar, the officers and the chaplain into the saloon, while the vicar, a young man, would come running up the street and into The Bell, his cassock, which he had not had time to remove, fluttering behind him as he hurried along.

But the parishioners thought less of their vicar the more religion grew apace with the troops as a result of his ministrations to our battery, so that, tongues wagging slanderously, he threw off his cassock and became an army chaplain.

Whether our battery had a bad influence, by accepted standards or not, on parsons I cannot say. We had only arrived in a remote Pennine village, right after the Dunkirk episode, when we all paraded to church in the usual way. The battery commander and I sat at the end of the pew by which the choir had to pass on its way out of the chancel at the end of the morning service. The vicar, on reaching us, leaned over—" Got a celebration now, but will see you in the Crown to-night at seven o'clock," and then passed on to the vestry with his choir. He too did a power of good with the men, but everywhere the gossips deplored to me, at the tea-parties to which we officers were invited, how their vicar had fallen in their eyes.

Yet both these men, and all the army chaplains I knew at all well, were in the direct line of that hearty, healthy parsonhood, which had carved in the gallery of its church :

> " God speed the plough
> And give us good ale enow . . .
> Be merry and glade,
> With good ale was this work made."

However, all this is a digression and now back to our subject. Because food and drink have always been the centres of good fellowship, we have records of feasts throughout all antiquity, and religion itself centres around the same gatherings. In our own religion we have numerous feast days which in the old days were real feasts, and the central point of all our ceremonial is based upon a communion service with its bread and wine—commemorating the last meal of Christ.

Therefore as our fellowship with God and man centres around the cup and the board, these subjects deserve no slight attention, much as they may be neglected to-day; and as the English cup was of old the *Mazer* cup, and as it was filled with the honey drink, *Mead*, we will, without more apology, turn to the consideration of *Wassail ! in Mazers of Mead.*

G. R. G

CHAPTER I

HONEY AND MEAD IN ANCIENT MYTHOLOGY

ALTHOUGH we may little realize it to-day, when the world was young, when the gods walked the earth and communed with men, and when men had more ready access to paradise than they have had since, mead was the liquor drunk by gods and men alike.

Among the ancients mead was not merely drunk as a wine, a liquor to refresh and stimulate, and therefore valuable as such, but it was also partaken of as something which in itself had magical and indeed sacred properties. As a result, it comes about that we find mead, its raw material honey, and even the creature which provides it, the bee, all holding high places in the sacred mythologies of olden times. Thus honey was considered a " giver of life ", and the bee was associated with the souls of men, and was a messenger of the gods. Honey was believed to have come down from Heaven as a dew, and was gathered from the flowers by the bees. This idea is to be found throughout the Vedas (the sacred books of the Hindus dating from 1500–200 B.C.), in Hesiod and Aristotle (Greek writers of the eighth and fourth centuries B.C., respectively) and in the Latin Virgil (70–19 B.C.), as well as in the Bible.

In those ancient hymns, written down in Sanskrit upwards of 5000 years ago by the Aryans before they entered and conquered India, known as the *Rig-Veda* we find that Krishna and Indra are called *Madhava*, meaning the honey-born ones, and their symbol was the bee. Consistent with this was the belief that in heaven there was a spring of mead—

" In the wide-striding Vishnu's highest footstep,
There is a spring of mead." [3]

It is a motif throughout ancient Aryan religions to find that the god, or his bird, steals the divine mead from heaven. Thus in ancient Indo-Aryan religion we find the eagle of Indra (in the *Vedas*), the Eagle of Zeus in Greek mythology, and Odin in the shape of a bird, in our own ancestral legends. But the myth is not restricted to the Aryans, although it is common to them, and probably more rightly is associated with them than with any other group of peoples. It is to be found among the Finns, where there existed the belief that high in the sky was the storehouse of the Almighty, containing the heavenly honey, which had the power to heal all wounds.

In the *Vedas* this mead (*madhu*) becomes confused with the sacred drink called *soma*, which had the same properties as the mead, which would seem to precede it in time. In the *Rig-Veda* we read that having drunk *soma*, immortality was obtained.[4]   This conception is certainly one associated with mead, as we shall see time and again.

This *soma* was made by the Indo-Aryans after they reached India, and it would appear to have been compounded from the yellow juice of some mountain plant mixed with milk, barley meal and honey. It will be shown later that mead liquors have frequently been adulterated with malt (from barley) and so this development from pure mead to *soma* is what is to be expected. Furthermore, among the Celts, for instance, the juice of the hazel, considered a magic milk, was also added. Milk of animals, also, has actually been used from time to time, by Poles and Celts in making some of their meads and metheglins.[5] Different, therefore, as *soma* was from the original mead, it was a derivative of it, and inherited the properties of the original sacred liquor. That this was so is clearly indicated by the fact that in many of the Vedic hymns *soma* is actually called by the old name of *madhu* (mead).

Among the ancient Hindus we find that *amrita* was another magical liquor, and was the immortal essence of the *soma*. Another such essence (or was it the same?) was *haoma*, a drink of the gods which we find in the *Avesta*. It is certainly probable that *haoma*, like *amrita*, was a variant of *soma* and so a form of mead.

Among the western Aryans, as we have already seen, whether among the Greeks or the Norsemen, there was the magic mead. Just as the eastern Aryans gave other names to it, such as *soma* and *amrita*, as time passed, so we find this magical liquor among the Greeks being referred to as *nectar* and *ambrosia*. There is some confusion between the two terms. Some of the ancient writers refer to *nectar* as a liquor (mead) and the others to *ambrosia* as a food, while others entertain quite the opposite notions. Zeus, for instance, was fed upon the sacred *ambrosia* brought by the seven doves (the Pleiades) from the western ocean. Homer certainly treats *ambrosia* as a food of the gods, although Sappho talks of goblets crowned with *ambrosia*, which clearly would suggest a liquor. Likewise Virgil considered it a drink, as we find in the *Aeneid* [6] where the wounds of Aeneas were cured when Venus " sprinkles health-giving juices of ambrosia " upon them : and again [7] it is in the same sense that he uses the term when he writes in the *Georgics* of Cyrene—" so she speaks, and sheds abroad an odorous stream of ambrosia ".

The confusion between *nectar* and *ambrosia* is probably more apparent than real. That both were derived from honey is certain. If the one of these which was a food (be it *nectar* or *ambrosia*) were only honey, or perhaps the equivalent of a mead-posset, having the sort of consistency of the Dutch liqueur *Advokaat* which is eaten in Holland with a spoon out of a glass, it would account for it being treated in some contexts as a food, and in others as a liquor, and so in later times lead to endless confusion.

Anyway, whether this heavenly drink of the Greek gods be called *nectar* or *ambrosia* matters little, it was undoubtedly a mead liquor, related to the *soma* of the eastern Aryans and the magic mead which Odin stole.[8]

It will be shown later that in the very nature of things mead-making preceded wine among the Aryans, and that is probably true for most if not all peoples. This antiquity would, apart from certain qualities connected with mead, tend to elevate it to great regard in the myths of the Aryan peoples, although we shall see later that its very specific properties were bound to leave a lasting impression upon the folk-memory.

Owing to the great gap in time between their general use of mead and the written accounts which we find in Greek and Latin sources it is understandable that references to mead in classical documents tend to be fewer than would otherwise be the case. Nevertheless they are to be found, and what is more in such context that it is clear that mead was the original liquor of the race, and of the gods.

Thus we read in Plato [9] that " After supper Poverty, observing the profusion, came to beg, and stood beside the door. *Plenty being drunk with nectar, for wine was not yet invented*, went out into Jupiter's garden, and fell into a deep sleep." In the Orphic myth we find that Kronos was made drunk by Zeus with honey, for " *wine was not* ". One of the names of Zeus, *Melissaios* (meaning, the one belonging to the bees), points in the same direction. Porphyry [10] also tells us that the ancients made their sacrifices with honey (that is, presumably, with mead) before they made them with wine. From Plutarch [11] we learn the same thing, that mead, before the cultivation of the vine, was the libation before the gods, and he goes on to add that foreign nations which did not drink wine still drank mead.

In the light of these facts it is significant to find that when Odysseus wished to call up Teiresias, the seer, he was told by the enchantress Circe, to make libations for the dead, *first* with mead and *afterwards* with wine. [12]

Although the secular use of mead is, understandably, not a matter of common reference in ancient authors it does occur. Thus we find in Apollonius Rhodius (235 B.C.) that the Argonauts drank mead, which was provided for them in large quantities by their cup-bearers, who bore it to them in full goblets. We also learn that a cup of mead was poured

upon the sea before the anchor was weighed—a custom probably not unrelated to our use of wine on the launching of a
ship.

Not only, however, was it known to the ancients in the
Mediterranean lands that mead had been the original wine
of their ancestors and of their gods, and was used in the
libations of the gods in former times, but, despite the abund-
ance of wine with which they were surrounded, it was still
in use for certain sacrifices (and even for banquets, as we shall
see later) till quite late in their history.

An example of this late survival is to be found in Alciphron,
in his letter, *The Courtesans*, where we read—

" So we began at once to prepare for the sacrifice. A little way
from the farm buildings, there is a rock, its summit shaded by plane
trees and laurel bushes and with myrtle thickets growing on either
side. All along the surface of the stone run strands of ivy clinging
in close tendrils, and from above falls a trickle of clear water. Just
where the rock projects some statues had been placed, Nymphs and
a Pan stooping forward as though he were spying upon them. We
built a rough altar facing them, and laying some sticks upon it to
make a blaze, we began by sacrificing a white hen. *Then we poured
out some mead* and lit a cake of incense in the fire and prayed earnestly
to the Nymphs—but just as earnestly to Lady Aphrodite as well—
that we might get a good bag of lovers." [13]

It is possible that in such a case as this, where the libation
was connected with prayers to Lady Aphrodite, the Great
Mother Goddess, or Bacchus or Dionysus, that mead rather
than wine might be used. There were special reasons why
this should be so.

Not only was mead the great wine of antiquity and the
liquor of the gods throughout the whole Aryan world, but it
also became associated with (if it had not been so from the
beginning) those cults in the Mediterranean which would
seem to have had a native origin rather than an Aryan, such
as the worship of Dionysus or Bacchus, who was the same god
as the Egyptian Osiris, and intimately connected with the
worship of the Great Mother.

Apart from its regard among the Aryans as a god-like

drink, which might have induced non-Aryan religious ceremonial to adopt it, and make it its own, there was a specific
reason why these cults should esteem it highly in their ritual.

From the earliest times men have recognized that honey,
and particularly mead, have strong revitalizing qualities, as
well as merely healing virtues. As a consequence of this it
was believed to be an elixir to prolong life, and this, no doubt,
is why the magic mead of heaven was believed to confer
immortality upon the mortals who partook of it. That is
why the Scots have a saying that mead-drinkers have as
much strength as meat-eaters, and the Germans have the
saying—*Bienen kommen eben so weit als Baren*, meaning that
mead is as strong, or strengthening, as meat. The passage
quoted from *The Georgics* was one in which Cyrene shed the
ambrosia over her son in order to fill him with god-like vigour.

But more than this. Early the strong aphrodisiac qualities
of the liquor were appreciated. Mead not only made for
strength, virility, and length of life, but also re-creative
powers. Nor were these ideas restricted to the Mediterranean
lands. We find that the Hindus, for instance, eat old honey
for increase in their virility.[14] While among our own Gothic
ancestors it was the custom at marriage, and for a month
afterwards, to feast upon mead, as a consequence down to the
present time we call the period following the wedding, the
honeymoon, and the French the *lune de miel*.[15] The Moors,
apparently, also considered honey as a love-stimulant. Beck
and Smedley remark upon this, that their wedding celebra-
tions were sex-orgies in which the guests were given honey
and " honey-wines " until they were drunk, because they
believed that honey had powerful aphrodisiac qualities.[16]

Now these native Mediterranean cults were concerned with
that basic principle—death of the outworn, the fertilization
of mother earth, of the whole of creation, of animals and of
every living thing, re-birth and growth. This was particularly so in the cult of Dionysus and in the worship of the
Great Mother Goddess, under whatever guise they appear.

A further piece of evidence of the association of mead and

honey with the Mother Goddess is provided for us by Virgil
in his *Georgics*, where he tells us that the beating of cymbals
to cause a swarm of bees to alight was in honour of Aphrodite
—" and all about raise tinkling sounds, and rattle the cymbals
of the mother of the gods." [17]

How many of the cottagers frantically beating their pots
and pans to make their swarms alight know that they are not
merely carrying out an ancient ritual of the bee-garden, but
taking part in some long-forgotten ceremonial of the clashing
cymbals of the temple worship of the Great Mother?

We get a quite late witness to the sexually strengthening
qualities of mead in Sir Kenelm Digby's *The Closet . . .
opened*, where he tells us of a worthy Burgomaster of Antwerp
in the seventeenth century, in discussing the recipe—*To
Make Excellent Meathe*. He says—

" This Meathe is singularly good for a consumption, stone, gravel,
weak-sight, and many more things. A chief Burgomaster of Ant-
werpe, used for many years to drink no other drink but this ; at
Meals and all times, even for pledging of healths. And though he
were an old man, he was of an extraordinary vigor every way, and
had every year a Child, had always a great appetite, and good
digestion ; and yet was not fat."

We get something similar to this in the *History of the
Principality of Wales*, by R. B. (London, 1695), where we
read—" Pollio Romulus, being an 100 years of age, told
Julius Caesar, that he had preserved vigour of his mind and
body by taking Metheglin inwardly and using oyl outwardly."

For these reasons alone mead and honey would be appropriate libations in the rituals connected with the Great
Mother Goddess, whose service was so intimately connected
with the procreation of all life. It is, therefore, not unexpected that the Courtesans, praying to the Great Mother, the
Nymphs and Pan [18] for lovers, should use mead rather than
wine for the libation at the altar.

It is also, as a consequence of such considerations, not
surprising to find that although Bacchus is traditionally the
god of wine, he was evidently the god of mead as well, and,

furthermore, his association with wine was later, and must
have come about as mead began to go out of common use
in the Mediterranean lands in which the cult flourished, and
where wine was so much more plentiful than mead could
ever be.

That mead was originally his sacred liquor seems to be
inferred by the fact that until the very end honey was always
sacred to the god, for his followers, the Maenads, carried ivy-
headed staves which streamed forth honey, and, according
to Ovid, he was credited with the foundation of bee-culture.

It is equally significant that the god of procreation, Priapus,
whose very name came to signify, when so used, the male
organ of generation, or again, a lustful man, had, according
to the Roman poet Calpurnius,[19] honeycombs sacrificed to
him.   According to the Greek poet Crinagoras,[20] in the
festival to Priapus and Pan mead was offered in the sacrifice.
(It is actually called " the ambrosia of the bees ".)   One
suspects that the Satyricon or love-potion with which the
priestess of Priapus, in her lewd dealings with the young men
in the inn was so free, on the Vigil of Priapus, was not
unrelated, in its derivation at any rate, to the sacred liquor
poured out to the god.   She was certainly very angry when
despite that, and the wine and the fine antepast laid on for
them, they did not come up to expectations and fell a nod-
ding.[21]   However, be that as it may, and to return to the
association of Pan with Priapus, and both with mead.   We
find that elsewhere, besides the instance just referred to, Pan
is called the saviour of the bees, and had honey sacrificed to
him.

It was probably this close association between the Great
Mother (and Priapus and Pan, and all else of that sort) and
mead, that accounts for surprisingly few references to honey
and bees in the Bible.   We know that the Bible writers must
have been familiar with apiculture.   Consequently it would
seem that it was perhaps due to the relationship of the bee,
and her produce, to Astarte or Ashtoreth, as the Great Mother
was called by them, which made it a matter of policy for the

scribes to avoid references as far as possible to a creature so involved in the ritual of a religion which they heartily disliked.[22]

It is to be expected that as mead ceased to be in general use, among those Aryans who had settled in the wine-producing lands of Greece, and adjacent parts, the patronage of Bacchus should be extended to the liquor which had gradually taken its place, and, as this occurred, some of the qualities of mead would come to be conferred upon its substitute. As wine is so like mead it must possess much the same characteristics, but there can be little doubt that the re-vitalizing powers are those particularly ascribed to mead rather than to wine. Consequently, when Apuleus,[23] having received a gift of wine from Byrrhena, at a time when he was making an assignment with the maid Fotis, says—" Behold how Bacchus the egger and stirrer of Venery, doth offer himself of his owne accord, let us therefore drink up this wine, that we may prepare ourselves and get us courage against soone, for Venus wanteth no other provision than this," he was really repeating traditional qualities associated with Bacchus as lord of mead rather than of wine.

In the same way that the qualities of mead came to be conferred upon wine, so often its very name (*nectar*) was given to the substitute, as nowadays we often, to be more polite, or to pay a tribute to the quality of the substitute, call margarine, butter ! After all, such a process was natural enough. A fine old wine lacking a superlative of its own found it in the word *nectar*. Thus we find it used in a passage of Theocritus—

" Meanwhile we broke the four-year-old seal from off the lips of the jars, and O ye Castalian Nymphs that dwell on Parnassus' height, did ever the aged Cheiron in Pholus' rocky cave set before Heracles such a bowlful as that ? And the mighty Polypheme who kept sheep beside the Anapus and had at ships with mountains, was it for such *nectar* he footed it around his steading—such a draught as ye Nymphs gave us that day of your spring by the altar of Demeter o' the Threshing-floor ? "[24]

We have already referred to Odin and the magic mead of heaven as an instance of the widespread connection among

the Aryans of mead with the gods. Since mead survived
longer in the north, where there was no vine to provide a
cheap substitute for it, it would be as well to dwell upon the
position of mead in remote times as we learn of it from ancient
northern mythology.

We discover that one of the rewards to the warrior for
reaching Valhalla was the draught of mead proffered to the
hero by the beautiful divine maidens. For, in the Prose
Edda, Gangler asked (no doubt with some concern) if water
was drunk in Valhalla, and Thor, in answer, reassured him
by asking if he believed that Kings and Earls would be
invited by the All-father to drink only water ! Men who had
suffered great hardships, wounds and pain, even unto death,
to reach Valhalla would have paid too great a price, if water
was their mead. No, from the goat Laerath there flowed such
plenteous mead that the heroes were fully satisfied of it.

The Celts also held to much the same view, for in their
Paradise there was a river of mead at which those who had
won through to immortality could refresh themselves.

These ideas of hearty Norseman and Celt were a trifle
different, as touching the Diety's hospitality, than is to be
found in some of the tee-total tracts !

The mead of our Anglo-Saxon forebears, according to their
mythology, gave the gifts of immortality, poetry and knowledge. It was for that reason that Odin drank up the magic
mead in three draughts and fled in the form of an eagle. Thus
he gained, presumably, not only immortality, but the gift of
tongues, wisdom and a knowledge of poetry. The latter, on
this account, came to be called Odin's gift, and poets were
known as the bearers of the mead of Odin.

As a result we read such a passage as that in the old poem,
the *Runahal*, which says—

> " A drink I took of the magic mead,
>   Taken out of Othrörir.
>   Then began I to know and to be wise,
>   To grow and to weave poems." [25]

This idea of mead conferring the gift of poetry is to be

found among the ancient Greeks, for surely it is inherent in the following lines from the old Sicilian poet, Theocritus—

" And I'll have him sing how once a king, of wilful malice bent,
   In the great coffer all alive the goatherd-poet pent,
   And the snub bees came from the meadow to the coffer of sweet
     cedar tree,
   And fed him there o' the flowerets fair, because his lip was free
   O' the Muses wine [i.e. nectar in the Greek] ; Comátas ! 'twas
     joy, all joy to thee ;
   Though thou wast hid 'neath cedarn lid, the bees thy meat did
     bring,
   Till thou didst thole, right happy soul, thy twelve months'
     prisoning." [26]

A consideration of mead in old mythology opens up into the whole field of the study of ancient religions, and the association therewith of the bee, a subject which, interesting as it may be, nevertheless would take us away from our main theme which is the discussion of mead itself from the earliest times.

It is, however, necessary to make one point. The peculiar properties of mead as probably the first wine drunk by man, and the qualities inherent within it, which have never been surpassed by the substitute liquors, all must have led men of the Aryan world, and no doubt the white peoples of the Hamitic and Semitic groups of people too, to a belief in the sacred character of not merely the liquor, but of the creature which bore the honey from which it was made. [27]

It is natural therefore to find that the bee was considered the messenger of God, [28] and no doubt from that arose the tradition of telling the bees of troubles and joys, a custom still current in country places to this day. The bee thus became a sacred symbol in many religions of the ancient world from which our own civilization has sprung. It was closely associated with the Great Mother Goddess, and it was figured in the mouth of the lion, in the religion of Mithra, and thereby was intended to represent the Word of God, or the Word proceeding out of the mouth of the god. In Chaldee the actual word " bee " is the same as " the Word ". [29]

Thus the very extensiveness of the symbology of the bee, and the ritual use of honey, in ancient ceremonial, is, in all probability, an indirect witness to mead, even in lands where we find little or no reference to it—for it should be remembered that it is only essentially in the Aryan world, rather than in the Semitic and the Hamitic which lay to the south of it, that we find the liveliest surviving conceptions of mead as the ancient liquor of gods and men, the giver of knowledge and poetry, the healer of wounds, and the bestower of immortality.   In these more southern lands direct and intimate contact with mead died much earlier than farther north, and so it is only by such rare survivals of older ideas, rituals and symbols, that we can trace its former existence.

CHAPTER II

ALE, MEAD AND BEER, BEFORE AND AT THE DAWN OF HISTORY

DRINK may be divided into five kinds. First we have various types of beers and ales, secondly there is mead, thirdly wine from grapes and other fruit juices, fourthly spirits, and lastly liqueurs.

FIG. 1

Ancient Egyptian Brewer

(After Wells, *Outline of History*)

Of these the first three are the earliest and ale and mead and their variants are the drinks of our own ancestors before wine was imported.

The old world (putting mead aside) can be divided into the ale-, beer- and wine-making regions. Wine was, in the main, restricted to the Mediterranean basin, and outside of that, including Egypt and Babylonia, ale and beer were in general use.

Our earliest records of beer go back to 5000 or 6000 B.C. where we find it being made in Babylonia from barley and

barley and spelt.   In Egypt at about the same time we find
it was drunk extensively by all classes, from labourers to
women of the harem.   In both countries it was much used
in medicines, having added to it bitter spices.   The code of
Hammurabi, one of the earliest law-givers in the world, living
about the end of the twenty-third century B.C. legislates upon
the sale of beer.[30]

The following are examples from this early code : [31]

"108.   If a (female) beer-seller [32] has not accepted corn as the
price of drink, but silver by the full weight has accepted and has
made the price of drink less than the price of corn, then that beer-
seller shall be prosecuted and thrown into the water.

"109.   If rebels meet in the house of a beer-seller and she does
not seize them and take them to the great house, that beer-seller
shall be slain.

"110.   If a priestess or holy sister who has not remained in the
convent shall open a beer-shop or enter a beer-shop for drink, that
woman shall be burned.

"111.   If a beer-seller has given sixty *qa* of drink on credit for
a festival, at the harvest she shall receive fifty *qa* of corn."

From these curious, but no doubt necessary laws, we at
least learn that women were the owners of the beer-shops and
that on the whole they would seem to have been rather low
haunts.

Pliny and Herodotus both speak of the barley " wine " of
Egypt and Herodotus and Strabo have references to millet
and barley beer in Abyssinia and Nubia.   It was from the
Egyptians that the Greeks learnt the art of brewing, although,
as they lived in a wine country, so relatively difficult a process
as brewing had little appeal for them.   Xenophon also noted
that in Armenia they drank a barley beer in which the barley
still floated so that they had to suck it up through reeds.
He says of it, " The liquor was very strong unless one mixed
water with it, and a very pleasant drink to those accustomed
to it."   The accompanying illustration makes it evident that
earlier still, in Babylonia, beer was also sucked up through
tubes, so we may assume that it was much the same in Lybia,
as the beer Xenophon experienced in Armenia.

FIG. 2

Beer-Drinking through Tubes in Ancient Babylonia

FIG. 3

Bottling Beer by Syphon in Ancient Egypt

One of the first references to beer in the western world is to be found in Pliny.[33]

" The Western nations produce their inebriating liquors from steeped and distilled grain. The Egyptians also extract their liquors from the same materials ; and thus no part of the world is exempt from drunkenness. Moreover, these liquors are made use of neat, and not diluted, as is the custom with wine. But Hercules seemed only to produce fruit from the earth ; whilst, alas ! the wonderful shrewdness of our vices has shown us in what manner water may be made to administer to them."

This liquor to which he refers, like the beer of Xenophon in Armenia, was evidently a strong college type of brew— and therefore something leaning heavily towards a wine in strength. From Xenophon's remark (despite the statement of Pliny) it was probable that water was often added to these strong brews.

It will be shown later that the real difference between ale and beer is the absence or addition, as the case may be, of bitter substances such as hops, although this is a distinction now lost in the modern classification of barley liquors. A further distinction in olden times was the greater strength of beer. Judged by either of these standards the liquor of the Babylonians and Egyptians was strictly speaking a beer, and although Pliny does not specifically say that the malted liquor of the western world was infused with bitter herbs, we may conclude that it was since he likens it to the Egyptian beer.

At first sight it might be assumed that our own ale, derived from our Anglo-Saxon and Norse forebears, came from the same source originally as the Egyptian and Babylonian liquors. But there is some reason to doubt this, and in this lies the reason for beginning a discussion of mead with ale ! The Anglo-Saxon word for ale is a more primitive form of the same word, *ealu*, and the Icelandic is *öl*. A word obviously related to this is the old Prussian *alu*, which, however, does not mean ale at all but mead.[34]

This suggests that our English ale of the Middle Ages and back to the dawn of Anglo-Saxon and Viking history was

originally a form of mead. Furthermore, this view is supported by the fact that among the Finns, as we shall see
later in their folklore, a small quantity of honey was essential
in order to make the mead ferment. It is hard to escape the
conclusion that this is a survival of a distant association
between honey and ale.

Credence is given to this view by the fact that we find in
the Middle Ages it was expressly forbidden to place hops in
the ale,[35] and therefore we can assume that ale consisted of
three ingredients only, water, alcohol (produced from the
malt) and yeast. In these simple terms it comes nearer to
mead than beer except for its much less strength and the fact
that it is malt and not honey which produces the alcohol.
While on the other hand, the bitter substances were always
an essential ingredient of the ancient beers.

In support of this we must not overlook the fact that
Pytheas (fourth century B.C.) [36] describes our Anglo-Saxon
(or Gothonic-Kimric) forebears who lived around the Ems
as a people eating honey on their bread and making a drink
of honey and corn. This is obviously the transitional stage
between ale from honey and ale from the cheaper product,
grain. This practice lingered on in the Celtic countries where,
in addition to malt-made ale, a malt-and-honey-made liquor
was brewed till quite late under the name of bracket, of which
something will be said later. In further support of this view
is the traveller's tale told by Wulfstan to King Alfred, in
which he recounted to him that among the Esthonians there
was so much honey that the king and nobles counted mead
as nought, leaving it to the poor and the servants, while they
themselves drank mare's milk because beer was unknown
among them. The first part of the story is obviously the
exaggeration of the traveller, as it is unlikely that however
plentiful honey might have been the Court was composed of
abstainers ! But what is of importance in this story, is the
fact that the making of a malt drink (whether beer or ale)
had not yet become known to some of the peoples of the
north Baltic. Thus all the evidence seems to suggest that

the knowledge of malting was late in arriving in northern Europe, and furthermore, it is the later the farther we pass away from the Mediterranean.

Therefore, having regard to the fact that besides the ale originally having been made from honey, mead was extensively used, as we shall see shortly, until we have evidence to the contrary we may assume that in primitive Aryan society honey was the basis of drink, just as malt was in Babylonia and the grape in the Mediterranean.

But, and this is an important factor which has affected the whole history of mead and its related liquors, at the dawn of history the world was the same size as at present, the flowers were about as numerous (or more so, as there was no tillage), men were few and the bee population had already filled the earth. In those far-off times honey was available for mankind in greater quantity than at any time since. For, as soon as man began spreading over the earth, he multiplied in numbers, and began reducing the bee-forage by the cutting down of forest and the scratching of the earth's surface to grow himself grain. So it has gone on and man has increased and more forest and pasture has been turned over to the plough and the bees have been steadily reduced in numbers. Therefore it is clear that although honey was formerly a ready source of alcohol it became steadily more difficult to obtain, and, in civilized society, its price has steadily increased.

Assuming that our early Nordic forebears made their drink in the form of mead from honey, we should expect, because of this increase in the cost of honey, to find a marked tendency to add more and more water to eke out the honey. This was the beginning of a lighter and relatively less intoxicating drink than mead—and so *ale* came to exist as apart from the stronger drink, or wine, called mead. But the word *ale* was probably the original word for all forms of mead, and so it has still survived in old Prussian.

Because of the gradual shift of the old word for mead (*ale*) to the weaker honey liquor it became necessary for a special word to be found to refer to the stronger liquor which we now call mead. It is natural that since mead was made from much more honey than ale that the old word for honey should be used to denote the stronger honey drink—and this word is *mead* itself. We have it in the Sanskrit as *mādhu* referring indifferently to honey or to mead, although by 3000 to 2000 B.C. it already had the meaning of mead.[37]

It is significant also that in Sanskrit the word *mādhu* means not only honey and mead, but also a " sweet drink ". This is clear from the following quotation from the *Rig-Veda* : [38] " I have partaken of the sweet food that stirs good thoughts, best banisher of trouble, the food round which all deities and mortals calling it honey-mead collect together."

In Greek the word *méthē* has the same significance because it was used for a strong drink, which is the same thing as saying a sweet drink, since all very sweet liquors make strong drinks, and all strong wines and honey liquors must have come from very sweet *musts*.

All this suggests that not only was there a former word for mead which might be that from which we derive the word ale, but that the word mead itself in ancient Aryan types when used for a liquor and not for honey, referred to a strong, even to dessert, type of drink.

To get over the difficulty that the word μέθη (*méthē*) had to be used, as *mādhu* was in Sanskrit, for a strong, and often sweet, drink and also for honey, it became necessary to make the distinction between them. Thus it came about that a word related to *méthē*, μèλι (*mèli*) came into use to signify honey, and from this is derived the Latin *mel* and the French *miel*.

We may conjecture that our own immediate ancestors had the same difficulty to overcome. In Anglo-Saxon the original Aryan word had become *medo, medu*, meaning mead alone and not honey. In Dutch, old Frisian, and Low German, it had become *mede*, in Norwegian *mjød*, Swedish *mjöd*, and in Danish *mjød*, and in Old High German *metu* or *mitu*, and in German *met* or *meth*. But the Anglo-Saxon nations did not resort to the primitive Greek solution of varying the root word. Instead a new word came into currency for honey. Thus in Anglo-Saxon we find our modern word honey as *hunig*, in Norwegian it is *honning*, and in German *honig*.

Since, in Greece, however, *méthē* (μέθη) and its related word *méthu* (μέθυ) became used for more than mead (for all strong drinks and for wine respectively), a new word became necessary to refer to mead specifically, and this word was at first μελίκᾶτος (*melíkātos*) and in later times still another word was used, and this was ὑδρόμελι (*hydrómeli*), whence the Latin and French *hydromel*, and the Italian *idromele*. Latin seems to have undergone the same development since the word *temētum* (which contains the root *met* or mead) came to mean any intoxicating drink and also wine.

It will be seen at once that this is the same process as that which took place among the Gothonic peoples with a difference of emphasis. In the Mediterranean basin, where the vine by extended cultivation provided an ever-increasing supply of wine, mead, which was derived from an ever-decreasing supply of honey, soon passed out of any commanding position in the life of the people, and survived mainly in tradition, as an expensive and rarely used libation to the gods (an instance of which we have already seen in Alciphron's *Courtesans*), and at the tables of the very wealthy alone.

An instance of this latter survival, where mead is brought on to be luxuriant and ostentatious, is provided for us in Petronius' account of the wicked old rascal and up-start Trimalchio, who with his bawdy wife threw large dinner-parties which lasted for days at which the whole of the degenerate lavishness of Roman life was displayed, and by which the host, Trimalchio, ex-slave and self-made man of rank and title, no doubt, paid his way in society.

" Then came a sumptuous Antepast ; for we were all seated, but only Trimalchio, for whom, after a new fashion, the chief Place was reserv'd. Besides that, as a part of the Entertainment, there was set by us a large Vessel of *Metheglin*, with a Pannier, in the one part of which were white olives, in the other black ; two broad Platters covered the Vessel, on the brims of which were Engraven

Trimalchio's Name, and the weight of the Silver." [Trimalchio was *nouveau riche* all right !]

He was lavish and generous to a degree, and pressed his guests to the Metheglin—" On this Trimalchio stopped his play for a while, and requiring the like for himself, proclaim'd, if any of us would have any more Metheglin, he was at liberty to take it."

Nothing was too good for such a banquet, and the Metheglin must have been rated among the great things in the realm of liquor for it was followed by the greatest of wine—

" and thereupon large double-Ear'd Vessels of Glass close Plaistered over, were brought up with the Labels about their Necks, upon which was this Inscription :

OPIMIAN MUSCADINE OF AN HUNDRED YEARS OLD." [39]

However, to return to the point. As a result of this ever-increasing scarcity of mead in the wine-growing lands of the Mediterranean the original word *méthē* came to mean all strong drinks (and not strong, or dessert, mead alone), while its slightly changed form μèλι (*mèli*) came to mean honey. Thus a specifically new word (and so first *melikātos* and later *hydromel*) became necessary to denote that honey wine which was of little general importance in the life of the common folk. Now, in contrast, among our ancestors things were different. Living as they did between Turkestan and the North Sea they were outside the lands producing ever-growing plentiful supplies of natural wine from grapes, and so mead was their only wine. As a result, it was unthinkable to those doughty heroes of Valhalla that the wine should seek for a name— honey was mead and mead was honey, that was the God-given relationship, and if you wished to differentiate your honey as honey from mead then a new name became necessary, not for this nectar of the gods, but for the raw material— honey.

While these developments were taking place in the Aryan world which led to the making of two types of liquor—mead and ale—there lay to its south in Babylonia, Egypt and probably further afield in western Asia, a region of genuine beer production, which was destined to influence the Aryan ale very considerably.

As the cost of honey continued to rise it became ever more difficult to produce the genuine ale from honey and at some period unknown to us, probably in prehistoric times, the introduction of malt as a substitute began to take place. Whether from Egypt or Babylonia or discovered independently we cannot tell, but more likely by the spread of the knowledge from either one of these great centres of civilization. Contact, directly and more frequently indirectly, was not rare in prehistoric times between the northern world and the south, as archaeological investigations now make very clear. The change over from mead to *soma*, which was made from barley, as the magical drink of the ancient Aryans probably indicates the time when this substitution of malt for honey was beginning to take effect among some of the ancient Aryans.

Anyway the knowledge that malted barley would act as a substitute for honey in the ale altered the whole survival outlook of ale, otherwise it would probably have been as rare a drink to-day as mead. Here, as in the case of the wine of the Mediterranean, man could master nature. He only had to plant more barley and he had more liquor, and as the population increased so did the barley tillage.

Therefore, at the dawn of history in northern Europe there are two well-defined types of drink. One is of a wine type, commanding all the respect of a wine, and that is mead, and the other is a long thirst-quenching, mildly cheering and warming liquor called ale. Mead was for the great and grand occasions, for the temple and the ceremonial, ale was for the masses and for all times.

CHAPTER III

THE ALE AND MEAD OF OUR ANGLO-SAXON AND NORSE ANCESTORS

IT is not now undesirable to turn to some of the passages in the old writers in which reference is made to ale and mead, so that from them we may be able to trace their development and character from the beginning of north European history until we are led to consider, as a result, in a later chapter, beer and sack, or sack-mead. From these passages we will also gain some incidental appreciation of the drinking habits and customs of our forebears which may not come amiss.

We have already seen that malted liquors were in use as far north and west as Britain in the time of Pliny. But these we have concluded, both from the heavy strong character of the liquor as described by him, and also from the comparison of it with the Egyptian drink, were beers.

When we turn to the *ancient* Germans (in part, at any rate, our ancestors) we find also a malted liquor described by Tacitus in the following words : " The liquor commonly drunk is prepared from barley or wheat, which, being fermented, is then brought to resemble somewhat wine." [40] Apparently our forebears even at this early time (end of the first century A.D.) were inclined to drunkenness, for he says : " The same abstinence [which they show in regard to food] is not observed with regard to the bottle. For if they are indulged in drunkenness to the extent of their desires, they may be as effectually conquered by this device as by arms."

Is this declamation by Tacitus merely abusive against his enemies or is it rooted in fact ? There is little doubt that the ale- and beer-drinking peoples of Europe to-day (and more so the spirit-drinkers) are more addicted to this vice than the wine-drinkers.

Anyhow, it is clear from Tacitus that the drink of the common man was probably ale. (The use of the expression " somewhat wine " suggests a less wine-like, and so less beer-like, drink than that noted by Pliny and Xenophon among more southerly and more westerly peoples.) But it should not be concluded that beer (a strong bitter drink) was unknown, as there are frequent references to it in Anglo-Saxon times, as we shall see later.

When we come to study our own northern records we are left with little doubt as to the great place of ale in the life of Anglo-Saxons, Danes and Norsemen. No event could take place without it, even if it had to be relegated to the lower orders because of the position demanded by mead on high occasions.

Beowulf, composed in the Anglian dialect of England about A.D. 700, is full of references to ale. We read of the drinking of ale, and the ale-benches on which it was drunk.[41] We also read of ale-bowls out of which it was quaffed, as in the following lines :

> " Full oft they boast, | with beer drunk
> Over the ale-bowls, | Did my athletes,
> That in the beer-hall | they would abide
> Grendel's onset | with grim swords." [42]

> " Then for the Geat-men | gathered together
> In the beer-hall | a bench was numbered ;
> There to sit | stout hearted went they,
> Assured in their strength | a thegn did service,
> He that bare in his arms | the ale-bowl beautiful,
> Poured the pure drink." [43]

> " At times before the doughty | the daughter of Hrothgar
> To the earls at each end | the ale-cup bore,
> ' Freawaru ' then I, | by the floor-sitters,
> Heard her name-d, | as the nail-studded treasure she
> Bent to the brave." [44]

In the same Anglo-Saxon accounts there are frequent references to mead.

In *Beowulf* we find the hall where the kings and thegns banqueted is called often the " Mead-place " [45] and the " Mead-Hall ".[46] For example : [47]

> " . . . | It was borne on his mind
> That a Hall house | he would have
> Made him by men | a mightier mead-place
> Than men's offspring | remembered ever,
> And there, inside | he would deal out to all,
> The young with the old, | as God had endowed him,
> Save the folk-share | and the fates of men."

As in the case of ale, the word mead is coupled with benches, and so we get mead-benches.[48] These benches were presumably ornamented by gold, for we read : [49]

> " . . . Then from the sills fell
> Mead-benches many | (my story tells)
> With gold finished, | Where the foes grappled."

As in the case of serving the ale, and we can presume more so since mead was saved for finer occasions and company, there was much ceremony associated with its service. Thus we read of Beowulf being given the mead-bowl or cup by Queen Wealtheow, after she had first passed around the flagon (of either mead, beer, or ale) to all and sundry.[50]

> " . . . | Went Wealtheow forth,
> The Queen of Hrothgar, heedful of custom,
> Gold decked she greeted | the grooms in hall :
> And that free-born wife | the flagon handed
> First to the East-Danes' | friend and Elder,
> Bade him be blithe | at that beer-tasting,
> Him, loved of his landsmen ; | he lustily took
> The feast and the flagon | fortunate King.
> Then went around | that Woman of the Helmings,
> To old and young, gave each his share
> Of the treasure-cup | till the time was come
> That she to Beowulf | braceleted Queen,
> Noble-minded | the mead-bowl bore ; "

Another quotation may be cited of a like kind from *Beowulf*: [51]

> " . . . | With mead-draughts moved
> Over that hall-floor | Halreth's daughter ;
> She loved the laity, | liquor-bowls bore
> To the hands of the heroes."

From Geoffrey of Monmouth [52] we have, not only con-firmation of this custom of the " hostess " bearing the drink to the guests, but, in addition, the toast words which accom-panied the act.   We thus read of a cup of " wine " (mead) [53] being given to the British king Vortigern by the daughter of Hengist, the Saxon :

> " And after that he [King Vortigern] had been entertained at a banquet royal, the damsel stepped forth of her chamber bearing a golden cup filled with wine, and coming next the King, bended her knee and spake, saying : ' Laverd King, wacht heil ! '   But he, when he beheld the damsel's face, was all amazed at her beauty and his heart was enkindled of delight.   Then he asked of his inter-preter what it was that the damsel had said, whereupon the inter-preter made answer : ' She hath called thee " Lord King " and hath greeted thee by wishing thee health.   But the answer that thou shouldst make unto her is " Drinc heil ".'   Whereupon Vortigern made answer : ' Drinc heil ! ' and bade the damsel drink.   Then he took the cup from her hand and kissed her, and drank ; and from that day unto this hath the custom held in Britain that he who drinketh at a feast saith unto another, ' Wacht heil ! ' and he that receiveth the drink after him maketh answer, ' Drinc heil ! ' "

One of the facts concerning mead is that, unlike some intoxicants, it is not a depressive.   This joyous character of mead comes out in some of these ancient accounts of the drink.   This is what we read of it in *Beowulf* :

> " The laity laughed ; | nor in all my life saw I
> Under heaven's vault, | among sitters in hall,
> More joy in their mead." [54]

Besides the mead and the ceremonies connected with its service, we read of mead-plains and mead-walks :

> " . . . | Fared soldiers many,
> Haughty-hearted, | to that high hall,
> To see a strange wonder ; | so himself too, the King,
> Out of the bride-bower, | the bracelet-store's warden,

Trod forth triumphant, | with a troop beyond the number,
He, kenned and chosen, | and his Queen beside him
The mead-walk measured | with her maiden-band." [55]

. . . .

" . . . | their Guardian with them,
Proud-minded among his troop | the mead-plains trod."

. . . .

What the mead-walks and mead-plains were is hard to say now. They may have been well-flowered parts of the country, or actually even (in the case of the mead-walks) bee-gardens where nectar was collected by domesticated bees. Or again, they may have been places where the herbs were grown, which, it will be shown anon, at a later stage of history, if not earlier, were added to the *must* in making that kind of mead called metheglin. In that case these mead-walks were what were later called in England hort-yards, or herb-gardens. It is in this sense of herb-gardens that Scott Moncrief [56] understands the expressions " mead-walks " and " mead-plains ". In the *Heimskringla, the Norse King Sagas* by Snorre Sturlason [57] we read of such herb-gardens having existed among our Norse forebears : " She dreamt, for one, that she was standing out in her herb-garden."

The *Heimskringla* [58] makes it clear that the ale of at least the period when the Sagas were written down (early thirteenth century) [59] was no longer made with honey but with malt. This is, of course, not surprising, since already we have learnt from Tacitus that grain was in general use in Germany for brewing 900 years earlier. The sole use of honey in making ale must have died out in prehistoric times. For we find that King Hakon (who lived in the tenth century, and who had become a convert to Christianity whilst his people were still pagan) " made a law that the festival of Yule should begin at the same time as the Christmas of the Church, and that every man, under penalty should brew a meal " (a maling or meal—a measure still used in Orkney) " into ale and therewith keep the Yule holy as long as it lasted ".

The *Heimskringla*, like *Beowulf*, is full of references to ale

and the high position it held in the lives of our Danish and
Norse ancestors, where it was as important as we have found
it among the Anglo-Saxons.

As in the case of the old English Parish Ales and merry-
makings, the Norsemen took their own ale with them to
festivals of a communal nature. So we read of a pre-
Christian sacrifice and festival of the time of Good King
Hakon in the Drontheim country : " To this festival all the
men brought ale with them." And later on we read of the
ceremonies associated with the sacrifice (but whether the
liquor drunk was ale or mead it is not clear) :

" . . . and he who made the feast, and was a chief [Earl Sigurd],
blessed the full goblets, and all the meat of the sacrifice. And first
Odin's goblet was emptied for victory and power to his king : thereafter, Njord's and Freya's goblets for peace and a good season.
Then it was the custom of many to empty the Brage beaker ; and
then the guests emptied a goblet to the memory of departed friends
called the remembrance goblet." [60]

The Brage beaker referred to was the bragging-cup, over
which boastful vows were made. The beaker or cup was
drunk in honour of the god of poetry, Brage. We have
another reference to this bragging-cup. A feast was attended
by six kings at the coming-of-age banquet (heirship feast) of
King Engjald, and it was held in a newly built hall in Upsala,
in Sweden :

" It was the custom at that time that he who gave an heirship-
feast after kings or earls, and entered upon his heritage, should sit
upon the footstool in front of the high-seat, until the full bowl, which
was called the Brage-beaker, was brought in. Then he should stand
up, take the Brage-beaker, make solemn vows to be afterwards
fulfilled, and thereupon empty the beaker. Then he should ascend
the high seat which his father had occupied ; and thus he came to
the full heritage after his father." [61]

Our Norse forebears were so addicted to drinking a goblet
of mead or ale to Odin, and then to Njord and Freya, that
the Christian Church was unable to abolish the custom, and
for centuries it was the custom on solemn occasions to drink
to the Almighty and the heavenly hosts ! The form of such
a toast is given by de Scala (*Life of S. Wenceslaus*) : " Let

us drink this cup in the name of the holy Archangel Michael, begging and praying him to introduce our souls into the peace of eternal exaltation."

Besides the ceremonial use of ale and mead on the great occasions, such as those at which an Earl made a sacrifice, or at which a Christianized Norseman took over into Christianity his pagan Yuletide habits or when a king drank the cup of Brage on his ascent of the throne, the cup was intimately associated with almost every phase of life. Thus it is we read of the " farewell ales " of which men must partake before departure and which was the forerunner of our now sadly declining custom of the " stirrup cup ". Such customs made life more gracious even in the rough days of the Vikings than it would have been otherwise— " When they were drinking the farewell ale—and they drank bravely—much and many things were talked over at the drink-table." [62]

From these facts it is clear that the cup of ale or mead and the board held a central position in the religious and ceremonial life of our ancestors both before and after they were Christians, no great or small occasion being complete without some ceremonial usage connected with them.

We frequently read of the Norsemen and the Anglo-Saxons drinking on benches before the fire (which was in the middle of the room) and it was actually across the fire that the drink was served. These benches were no doubt the ale-benches referred to in *Beowulf*, and they were as an essential part as the goblets, horns and bowls to the whole furnishing of drinking. These customs began to change in Norway, however, in the eleventh century, when King Olaf the Quiet brought in the revolutionary idea of building chimney-places in all the rooms—a change which had already taken place elsewhere—and so the ale- and mead-benches ceased with the fire, to be the centre of the life of the household. *Heimskringla* tells us of this change :

" It was the fashion in Norway in old times for the King's high seat to be on the middle of a long bench, and the ale was handed across the fire; but King Olaf had his high seat made on a high bench across the room; he also first had chimney places in the rooms and the floors strewed both summer and winter." [63]

Interesting as the account of the ale-drinking of the Norsemen may be, the *Heimskringla* throws some added light upon the more important central theme of mead—since any discussion of other wines and liquors in these pages is only made so far as it is necessary to wring out every drop of wisdom upon mead and its culture.

We learn that, as in *Beowulf*, where the queen bears him the mead, mead was usually drunk from the mead-bowl (whatever other vessels were used from time to time). This may be of some importance, as there is reason to believe that the mazer bowl was the traditional vessel from which mead was drunk at a later period. But this is anticipating a future discussion. Here in *Heimskringla* we read such passages as:

> " And silent Tore sits and dreams
>   At home, beside the mead-bowl's streams." [64]

>   .   .   .   .

> " The bowl runs o'er with Odin's mead,
>   That fires the scald when mighty deed
>   Has to be sung . . ." [65]

>   .   .   .   .

The Odin's mead referred to in this verse is called Bodn, and it was the blood or mead that the sons of Brage, the god of the poets, drank in order to receive poetical inspiration.

From this Norse document we also glean some information of the way mead was made in the following interesting account of the death of King Fjolne, who was one of the proto-historic kings of the Norse and who by accident met a death not unlike that which was arranged for the unfortunate Duke of Clarence, when he was drowned in a butt of Malmsey wine.

" Once when Fjolne went to Frode in Sealand, a great feast was prepared for him, and invitations to it were sent all over the country. Frode had a large house, in which there was a great vessel many ells high, and put together of great pieces of timber; and this vessel stood in a lower room.   Above it was a loft, in the floor of which was an opening through which liquor was poured into this vessel. The vessel was full of mead, which was excessively strong.   In the evening, Fjolne with his attendants, was taken into the adjoining loft to sleep.   In the night he went out to the gallery to seek a certain place, and he was very sleepy and exceedingly drunk.   As he came back to his room he went along the gallery to the door of another loft, went into it, and his foot slipping, he fell into the vessel of mead and was drowned." [66]

It was the custom (or at any rate a marked tendency) in early society, and right down to the Middle Ages, to drink the wine young, when it was at its sweetest and strongest. Therefore, it is possible that this mead was drunk directly from the vat, without being stored in a form of cask. Incidentally, King Fjolne was not the only King who died in mead.   J. Magnus (*Historia Sveonum*) tells us of one Swedish King Hunding, who, having heard the false rumour of the death of his brother-in-law, Hading, King of Denmark, at a great feast to his nobility, threw himself into a large vessel of mead.

The laws of the Welsh King, Howel the Great (tenth century) would suggest that this was the case, for we find that he legislated upon the duties of the mead-maker and the butler, laying down the rule that the former should be responsible for the mead from the time he prepared it till he covered the vat, while the butler's started from the moment he began to drain it.   This, incidentally, lets us see that the procedure was to make the *must*, and leave it uncovered during the first fermentation.   This would account for King Fjolne's accident.   After being covered (or " stopped close " as the saying is), which occurred at the end of the first fermentation, the mead would then be allowed a greater or lesser time in which to develop as was thought fit by the circumstances of the time.   From such a vat, presumably in any state, from new to old mead, it would be drained direct into horn, mazer, goblet or cup.

As such huge vats, as the one at Sealand in which King Fjolne met his unexpected end, would take some time to drain (even granting the great retinues and armies of house-

carls who made it their business to drink the liquor) it would
be necessary to make it strong and sweet so that it should
keep while it was being drunk. With age most of these
liquors would become dry, but whilever they were drunk
new they were no doubt sweet.

Of course, mead could be made sufficiently strong to
remain sweet with age, so it is not possible to tell whether
a liquor described as sweet, was merely sweet because it was
of no age or not. The sweetness in mead was undoubtedly
looked upon as a favourable quality among our ancestors,
as sweetness in wine generally was held to be in early times.
This is seen from the Anglo-Saxon epic poem—*Finnsburgh*.

" Nor heard I ever that more worthily | in wars of men
Sixty battle heroes | bore themselves better,
Nor even did swains for their sweet mead | give seamlier payment
Than to Hnaef was paid | by his house-fellows.
They fought five days | yet fell there none
Of the doughty comrades ; | but the doors they held."

In the *Heimskringla* [67] there is another reference to strong
drink, under the year 1167, at a Candlemas feast—" The
priest gave Erling strong drink in the evening, and he let
him have an excessive quantity of it."

But whether this was strong mead is another question.
The passage itself does not enlighten us. We shall see later
that the Hebrew word for strong drink, translated in the
Vulgate as *Sicera*, is to be found in the Anglo-Saxon gospels
as beer.   On the other hand there is some doubt whether *beer*
means what we mean by the word, and we shall see later that
the word might quite conceivably refer to the stronger and
sweeter meads.

That the mead was not always new sweet wine is clear
from one of the ancient Norse Eddas,[68] where we read of the
mead being old.   In this account we find that Sif, the wife
of Thor, offers one of the gods, Loki, a goblet of mead with
these words :

" Hail to thee, Loki, and take thou here
The crystal cup of old mead."

This is important as it established the fact that by early Norse times the art of keeping the drink till it was old and matured had been discovered. Furthermore, it was recognized that this mead was the best, and that is why it is given to the gods. Civilization had been achieved. For to put liquor aside, to watch it, nurse it, and study its needs, till in the fullness of time it has achieved that bouquet which a well-kept age alone confers, demands a degree of civilization of no mean order. Such mead, if kept long enough, would rarely be sweet and must have been dry, unless the original *must* had been made very sweet.

There can be little doubt, from the evidence we have examined, that mead, in comparison with ale, was a strong drink which had a quality of sweetness, at some stage of its maturation (giving way, naturally, to dryness when old), in Anglo-Saxon and Viking times and right down to the twelfth century. This confirms the conclusion we had already arrived at from the etymological evidence where we saw that *méthē* (μέθη) in Greek meant a " strong drink " and *mādhu* in Sanskrit a " sweet drink ". The character of the mead had therefore remained unchanged for many thousands of years.

Of course there is much more we should like to know. Granted the wine was sweet and strong—but how strong ? Ale is after all a weak drink and one not particularly sweet. Therefore in comparison with ale new mead would be both sweeter and stronger, and old mead as sweet and very much stronger ; but this would not mean that mead was comparable with what we, to-day, call sweet wines. It is against this standard, " ale ", that we should draw our conclusions rather than against that of sweet and strong wines, such as Port and Sherry which are so often abnormally sweet and fiery, the latter characteristic being from fortification by spirits. That being so we must conclude that ancient mead ranged from the type of the sweeter French wines (such as the Graves to the Fargues, Barsacs, Sauternes, Bommes and Preignacs) to the very sweet wines, of the Sherry variety, of which more will be said later when we come to discuss sack.

And to achieve the latter type large quantities of an ever-increasingly expensive honey had to be used, so the tendency would be as time went on to make the mead drier, and, where sweetness was desired, to drink it new from the vat before all the natural sugars had undergone change in fermentation. Only among the wealthy would sweetness and quality be achieved together, by making the liquor strong, and then ageing it by keeping the mead till it was mature.

A possible reference to the practice of drinking new (and therefore sweet) mead is perhaps to be seen in the following account from the *Heimskringla* :

" The king (Harold) walked up and down the floor casting his eye along the benches ; for he had a feast in the house, and *the mead was just mixed*.

" The king then murmured out these lines :

" ' Tell me, ye aged grey-haired heroes,
Who have come here to seek repose,
Wherefore must I so many keep
Of such a set, who, one and all,
Right dearly love their souls to steep,
From morn till night in the mead-bowl ? ' " [69]

If this account refers not to newly fermented mead which had still much. of its sweetness, then it must refer to the mixing of herbs and spices into the wine. To this subject we will return later when we come to discuss the gruit of which we read in the Middle Ages, and which is an essential ingredient of the spiced mead called metheglin.

Not only in Norway, but in England itself mead was maintaining its premier position, despite the greater use of wine in the ages after the days of Beowulf, right up to the Norman Conquest.

Thus we read in *William of Malmesbury* that the monks of Glastonbury had on special occasions " mead in their cans, and wine in their grace-cup ". At Abingdon Monastery the noble founders' great bowl was used to fill the monks' drinking-horns twice a day with mead.[70] While we find, for example, that Ethelwold allowed his monastery on its festivals at dinner a sextorium (fifteen pints) of mead between six of the brothers, and for their supper the same quantity between twelve, while on certain of the great festivals he gave them a measure of wine.[71] Three and three-quarter pints could not be considered an ungenerous ration, even for the greatest festivals. This large ration suggests that the mead here, as in several other cases we have considered, was not a strong sweet drink of a high alcoholic content, but must have been nearer the strength of a dinner wine—in other words, nearer 11 per cent than 15 per cent alcohol, and if the monks had a good cellar and cellarman, it was old, and therefore dry.

There is also an interesting reference in the Anglo-Saxon poem *Judith*, which is based upon the Apocryphal book of that name. Here we read of Holofernes, the leader of the Assyrian army, getting roaring drunk on wine till:

> " exhilarated with wine ;
> in the halls of his guests,
> he laughed and shouted ;
> he roared and dinned."

And throughout the account we read of these Assyrians being drunken and sodden with wine.

But, when we come to the account of the slaughter of the wine-drunken Assyrian host, we read that they were mead-weary, indicating that mead and wine were liquors of equally high quality in the eyes of the Anglo-Saxons, and therefore loosely interchangeable terms. Thus :

> " Stern-mineded, they [the Hebrews] advanced
> with fierce spirits :
> they pressed on unsoftly,
> with ancient hate,
> against the mead-weary foe." [72]

We also learn that Harold Godwinson (who as King Harold died at Battle resisting the invasion of the Conqueror) prepared for a royal banquet at Hereford in the time of the Confessor and among the drinks provided were mead, wine, ale, pigment, morat and cider.[73] Pigment (the Pyment of Chaucer) and morat were both sweet wines related to mead and of which we shall treat later.

The *Ruin*, one of the finest Anglo-Saxon poems, also deliberately confounds mead and wine, in the same way as we have just seen in the poem of *Judith*. For here the poet, musing probably upon the ruins of Bath, and the Roman civilization which had once been there, speaks of the banqueting-hall as the *Mead*-hall. The use of the word mead is obviously as deliberate here as in the case of *Judith*, for the poet mentions wine in the same poem. In any case, we should remember that the Anglo-Saxons were not unaware of the use of the vine, as they had both vineyards [74] themselves and they were also in the habit of drinking imported wine as well.

This poem is so fine that it is worth quoting part of it :

" Wondrous is this wall-stone ; broken by fate, the castles have decayed ; the work of giants is crumbling. Roofs are fallen, ruinous are the towers . . . Often this wall, grey with lichen and stained with red, unmoved under storms has survived kingdom after kingdom . . . Bright were the castle-dwellings, many the bath-houses, lofty the host of pinnacles, great the tumult of men, *many a mead-hall full of the joys of men*, till Fate the mighty overturned that. The wide walls fell ; days of pestilence came ; death swept away all the bravery of men ; their fortresses became waste places ; the city fell to ruin . . . Wherefore roof is stripped of tiles ; the place has sunk into ruin, levelled to the hills, where in times past many a man light of heart and bright with gold, adorned with splendours, *proud and flushed with wine*, shone in war-trappings, gazed on treasure, on silver, on precious stones, on riches, on possessions, on costly gems, on this bright castle of the broad kingdom." [75]

We cannot leave the story of mead among our Anglo-Saxon forebears without quoting one of their riddles on mead. In the old times, when men sat around the hearth in hall, they spent much time in telling tales and asking riddles, and this is one of these, the answer to which is mead :

" I am cherished by men, found far and wide, brought from the groves and from the city-heights, from the dales and from the downs. By day wings bore me in the air, carried me with skill under the shelter of the roof. Afterwards men bathed me in a tub. Now I am a binder and scourger ; straightway I cast a young man to the earth, sometimes an old churl. Straightway he who grapples with me and struggles against my strength discovers that he must needs seek the earth with his back, if he forsakes not his folly ere that. Deprived of strength, doughty in speech, robbed of might, he has no rule over his mind, feet, nor hands. Ask what is my name, who thus on the earth in daylight bind youths, rash after blows." [76]

The riddle tells the origin of the mead, from nectar borne from the dales and downs on the wings of the bees. Then it explains how the mead is made, by taking the combs of honey and soaking them in water.

It is of interest to notice the emphasis which the author of the riddle lays upon those likely to abuse, to their cost, the mead which the bees have provided from their honey. It is mainly heady, unsteady youth, and when it is sometimes the old, it is an old churl, an ignorant, boorish, common fellow, whose undeveloped palate is as raw as that of youth.

The riddle also draws attention to the excess of mead going especially to the legs. This traditional effect of mead is commonly accepted among old country mead-makers, and it receives confirmation from Poland, where it is said that the abuse of the liquor " makes you drunk only from the waist downwards, with surprising effects upon strangers who discover they are drunk only when they attempt to rise ".[77]

The subject of the abuse of wine and mead is one often referred to by the Anglo-Saxon writers. In the *Fates of Men,* which is part of the Exeter Book (which also contains the *Ruin*) and which was given by Leofric, Bishop of Devon and Cornwall, Chancellor to Edward the Confessor, to the Cathedral at Exeter, we are told how the abuse of wine and mead will lead the intemperate man, sitting upon the mead-bench, to hasty words, causing him to receive the " sword's edge " which takes away his life, because " he knows not how to check his mouth with his mind ", and men call him a self-slayer, " and talk of the drinking of him who was roused by mead ". Thus a people who loved and cherished their mead spoke of its abuse. But in the same poem, they tell of it as a reward to the man of virtue who has lived well " by the strength of God ", who " later in old age [shall] become happy, enjoy days of gladness, and receive wealth, treasures and *the mead-goblet among his kinsmen* ".[78]

CHAPTER IV

MEAD AMONG CELT, SLAV AND FINN

FROM the widespread distribution of the word mead in all its variants throughout the Aryan world, it is clear that we ought not to limit our study of its use to our Anglo-Saxon and Norse ancestors in these islands. Their enemies, the British Celts in the West and the Slavs in the East, were not unacquainted with its use, and so far as the Britons were concerned, they held it in no less high esteem than did the court of King Alfred the Great or the earlier and ruder Harolds, Olafs and Beowulfs. Pliny, speaking of the British Celts, tells us that " these islanders consume great quantities of honey-brew " (mead). We also learn that it was drunk by the Gauls, in nearby France, where we learn they had a rich mead called *zythus* and a less generous one known as *corma*.

Britain was, of course, called, among the Celts, by the bardic name of the " Honey Isle of Beli " which, no doubt, not only referred to the quality of its honey, but had an oblique reference to the mead wine held in high esteem by the Celtic nations.

One of our principal sources of information on Celtic mead lies in the *Mabinogion* and related documents. Since these were written down in the Middle Ages, after they had often been handed down for many generations by oral tradition, they obviously relate to much earlier times. The romance of Taliesin, for instance, probably goes back to the sixth century and is contemporary with King Arthur.

In " The Lady of the Fountain ", one of the tales in this collection which is of a later date, when the stories of Arthur had become part of the literature of Europe, we have an interesting reference to mead as the drink of kings. We may assume, therefore, that it reflects in some measure not merely the traditional estimation and regard for mead, but also that of the Middle Ages, particularly around the thirteenth and fourteenth centuries, when wine was already accessible to the great and used by them. Bearing that fact in mind, it is clear that in the mind of the Welsh bard it was still rated as a liquor of worth, fit to have all its own paraphernalia of cellarage and cellarman.

" King Arthur was at Caerlleon on Usk ; and one day he sat in his chamber ; and with him were Owain the son of Urien and Kynon the son of Clydno, and Kai the son of Kyner ; and Gwenhwyvar and her hand-maidens at needlework by the window. . . .

" In the centre of the chamber King Arthur sat upon a seat of green rushes, over which was spread a covering of flame-coloured satin, and a cushion of red satin was under his elbow.

" Then Arthur spoke : ' If I thought you would not disparage me,' said he, ' I would sleep while I wait for my repast ; and you can entertain one another with relating tales, and can obtain a flagon of mead and some meat from Kai.' And the King went to sleep. And Kynon the son of Clydno asked Kai for that which Arthur had promised them. ' I, too, will have the good tale which he promised to me,' said Kai. ' Nay,' answered Kynon, ' fairer will it be for thee to fulfill Arthur's behest, in the first place, and then we will tell thee the best tale that we know.' So Kai went to the kitchen and to the mead-cellar, and returned bearing a flagon of mead and a golden goblet, and a handful of skewers, upon which were broiled collops of meat. Then they ate the collops and began to drink the mead." [79]

We learn that the King's mead-cellar was under the direct care of the Steward of the Household, who was the chief officer of the Court,[80] which is further evidence of the regard for what was undoubtedly a royal drink. The mead-maker, too, was an important personage in the time of Howell the Good (tenth century). He had free lands, horse, clothing, and lodging in hall with the steward provided in return for the exercise of his craft.

Even the size of the vats was standardized ! At any rate, it was when the mead concerned entered into transactions connected with what were tantamount to feudal dues.

Unlike the great vat that swallowed King Fjolne, these Welsh vats would appear to have been much smaller—being less than about twelve cubic feet or thereabouts.

As so much had to be paid in kind in those days it is interesting to learn that a mead-maker took one-third of the mead made for a customer as his own payment.

Such a vat as the one described was valued at 10s. What is the real relationship of this to our present money is hard to say. We might make an attempt to get some appreciation of it by taking the price of a swarm of bees, which was valued at 1s. 4d. Before the Second German War a swarm cost 35s., that is twenty-six times more than in those early times. Consequently the vat would cost £13 in our money : or allowing for the inflation prevailing as a consequence of the war, somewhere about £40. Allowing for several deductions payable in kind (to the mead-maker and to the honey-producer), this would work out at a cost price of 10s. 6d. a gallon, or 1s. 7d. a bottle, pre-war, and, perhaps, now equal to about 5s. a bottle. This figure would seem to bear some relationship to our own costs, for it should be remembered that if duty and retailer's profit alone were added to the above figure it would bring the bottle up to a cost of 10s. : and of course nothing has been allowed for bottles, corks, wax, labels, and that abomination of modern life—advertising ! All these would surely run the cost up to about 14s. a bottle. However, the fact remains that our forebears, dispensing with all these impositions, and making their liquor locally, could afford to drink at 5s. what costs us upwards of half a guinea and more.

However, all this is a digression from the laws of Howell the Good one thousand years ago, in which detailed instructions are laid down for the whole practice of mead manufacture. From this we have clear evidence that by this time mead-making had become an art, regulated by custom and statute, and it was not at the mercy of anyone.

Such mead was the drink of kings and heroes. One old Welsh poem portrays the honoured warriors as wearing gold and drinking the liquor from golden goblets. Thus the bard, Aneurin, sings—

> " The Warriors who went to Cattraeth were renowned ;
> Wine and Mead out of golden goblets was their beverage.
> That year was to them one of exalted dignity,
> Three warriors and three-score and three hundred, wearing the golden
>   torques," etc.[81]

The splendour (real or imaginary) of Arthur's court causes the bards to harp upon mead as the drink of kings, princes and great warriors. Their poetic souls could not contemplate an Arthur drinking ale in the way the more realistic Anglo-Saxon writers could have done. There is a place for ale and there are places for mead and wine, as the writers of the sagas knew ; but the lofty Celtic bard's soul made his heroes live in the best romantic style of the time.

We have already seen, in the previous chapter, where Loki, the Scandinavian god, is offered " the crystal cup of old mead ", that one of the great qualities of mead is its sparkling brightness. This characteristic was no more missed by the ancient Celts than by the Anglo-Saxons and Norsemen. Aneurin, writing of the death of Caradawc, one of the battle knights of Britain at King Arthur's court, writes of it—

> " From Cattraeth and its carnage
> From the hostile encounter,
> After the clear bright mead was served,
> He saw no more the dwelling of his father ! "[82]

But the Celt, no less than the Anglo-Saxon folk, recognized the improvement in the liquor produced by ageing, and so we find, for instance, the ancient Ultonians (Scots), in *Diarmuid and Grainne*, talking of the satisfying qualities of old mead.[83]

The paleness of the mead, another of its qualities, is referred to in the same *Gododin* of Aneurin, to which reference has already been made, where he laments, as he does throughout this poem, the fact that his heroes got themselves drunk on mead before this battle of Cattraeth, and so were led to their slaughter.

> " They went to Cattraeth :
> Loquacious were their hosts.
> Pale mead had been their feast, and was their poison." [84]

To the Welsh bard Taliesin are we indebted for not only a fine account of mead, which raises an interesting problem, but also for what must be the most lengthy surviving extract left us by the ancients in praise of this princely liquor.

Taliesin was probably a real bard of the sixth century and contemporary with King Arthur. Therefore this is one of the earliest as well as one of the most interesting references now in our hands. It was sung on the occasion of Taliesin's plea to the king for the release of his master Elphin from prison :

> " I adore the Supreme, Lord of all animation,—
> Him that supports the heavens, Ruler of every extreme,
> Him that made the water good for all,
> Him who has bestowed each gift, and blesses it ;—
> May abundance of mead be given Maelgwyn of Anglesey,[85]
>   Who supplies us,
> From his foaming meadhorns, with the choicest pure liquor.
> Since bees collect, and do not enjoy,
> We have sparkling distilled mead which is universally praised.
> The multitude of creatures which the earth nourishes
> God made for man, with a view to enrich him ;—
> Some are violent, some are mute, he enjoys them.
> Some are wild, some are tame ; the Lord makes them ;—
> Part of their produce becomes clothing ;
> For food and beverage till doom will they continue
> I entreat the Supreme, Sovereign of the region of peace,
> To liberate Elphin from banishment,
> The man who gave me wine, and ale, and mead,
> With large princely steeds, of beautiful appearance ;
> May he yet give me ; and at the end,
> May God of his good will grant me, in honour,
> A succession of numberless ages, in the retreat of tranquillity.
> Elphin, Knight of mead, late be thy dissolution ! " [86]

We must allow for poetic licence and for the fact that the ancients had already espied the clear sparkling, in the sense of glittering, character of mead. But here we have in the same poem " *foaming* meadhorns ", and " *sparkling distilled mead* ". Is it possible that they were able to make mead sparkling (in the sense that champagne or cider is sparkling) at this time ?

It was a saying in ancient Wales, that three things were to be communicated to the King before all others :

1st, Every sentence of the judge ;

2nd, Every new song ; and

3rd, Every cask of mead.

No matter how highly wine may have been valued, and rightly so, up to the twelfth or thirteenth centuries it seems from the foregoing evidence clear that mead was the courtly drink of the Britons and Welsh.

When we realize the great place which mead and its raw material, honey, played in the civilization of ancient Britain we can begin to appreciate the significance of one of the poetic and ancient names for Britain—the Honey Isle.

Among the Irish (as may be gathered from the Ultonian reference to the satisfying qualities of old mead) the culture of the bee was as important as among the Welsh, and a large part of the native Celtic (Brehon) laws is devoted to it. Besides its use as a sweet and for cooking, its principal use was, as elsewhere, for making mead, and, perhaps, at an earlier cycle, ale too before the malting of barley had been discovered. At any rate up to the Middle Ages mead and ale were the two chief drinks of the Irish. In Gaelic poetry we read of the golden-haired Niamh describing paradise to Ossian, and saying—" Abundant there are honey and wine." [87] While a princess handed to the great Irish hero, Finn Mac Cumall, a silver cup filled with mead, with the words— " Mead, delectable and intoxicate." [88] Indeed, mead was in great request among them, and it was known as the dainty drink of the nobles, and the great royal hall of Tara, where the High-King of all Ireland ruled, was called the House of the Mead Circle.[89]

Even saints partook of mead. We find that St. Findian lived for six days a week on bread and water, but, on Sundays, he fed upon salmon and a " full of a cup of clear mead ". There are also connections between mead and the famous and popular St. Brigit, who, as Our Lord turned water into wine, changed vats of water into mead, and, even, on one occasion did something more remarkable. When the King of Leinster came to drink the mead prepared for him it could not be found. Whereupon St. Brigit, equal to the occasion, blessed the empty vessels which immediately filled with mead.[90]

A variant of mead was also drunk by the Gaels, and this was hazel mead. We read, in the seventh-century poem, *King and Hermit*,[91] of Marvan drinking this liquor, and Joyce [92] tells us of hazel mead drunk from cups of gold. Such mead would appear to be in the direct tradition of the Aryan *soma*. Elsewhere we have mentioned the Welsh habit in some cases of putting milk in the metheglin. This may be a further variant of the *soma* tradition.

Among the Slavs, and those peoples to the east and north of them, the Finnu-Ugrians, we find mead in early use. These non-Aryan peoples on the borders of the Aryan Slavs probably gained their knowledge of mead from them or other Aryan sources, since their words for honey or mead are indubitably of Indo-European origin. Thus we find the Finnish is *mesi*, the Mordvin is *med*, and the Magyar, *méz*, all words close to the ancient Aryan *Madhu*. As Hungarian tradition brings the knowledge of mead with them into Europe from Asia, it is likely they became acquainted with it from eastern Aryan sources.[93] By the ninth century mead was certainly the drink of the Esthonians, although they had not yet the knowledge of beer-making.[94]

Mead-making was flourishing at the same time in Poland, for we find that the Polish Prince Piast (A.D. 824), who lived to be 120, had a bee-garden near Keuschweitz in which he toiled himself, making his own mead, and offering it to his guests. There is a legend about this prince which illustrates the importance of mead in everyday life in Poland. As a poor peasant wheelwright, Piast was keeping a holiday on the birth of his son in a hut under the linden trees. Two strangers came to him claiming that they had been driven from the castle of the wicked Polish King Popiel. They were welcomed by the poor man, and seated at a table spread with the best which the young wheelwright could lay before them. In gratitude they baptized Piast's newly born son and told him that his granaries would ever be full of corn and his cellars of mead. And from that day he never wanted for bread or mead—for he had taken in angels unawares, and we suspect that it was they who were responsible later for elevating the young wheelwright to the throne of Poland.[95]

The important place that mead has always had in Poland is perhaps best summarized in the words of one of Henry Sienkiewicz's characters (Zagloba) in *The Deluge*—" The Lord God knew why he created bees."

Another royal bee-keeper was that great enemy of the Slavs, Charles the Great, who made a bee-garden in the woods around Nuremburg. Later, only fifty bee-masters were allowed to keep bees there. (Incidentally this shows how important woodlands are to bee-keepers, a fact often forgotten by some bee-masters who look to clover for their main source of nectar.)

The Rügen Slavs (who were not Germanized until later than the fifteenth century), according to Saxo Grammaticus, writing at the beginning of the thirteenth century, in the worship of their sun god, Swantovit, used mead in the temple ritual. The priest took the cup of mead from the hands of the idol, where it had been placed at the last harvest, and by the quantity of the mead in the cup he forecast the coming year. The mead was then poured out to the idol, and the ceremony included the priest drinking the mead and refilling the cup for the idol.

As we have already seen, another Slavonic people, the *ancient* Prussians, before they were half-exterminated and then Germanized, had the use of mead which they called *alu*, although their nearby Slavonic neighbours, the Poles, how-ever, used the word *miòd*, which is the same word as our mead.

We also find it recorded that the people of Transylvania, who were either Slavonic Vandals or some Gothonic folk, drank mead. For we learn that in the days of the terrible

Attila, when he and his flat-nosed, short, strong, sallow-faced warriors, invaded Europe, and spread all along the Roman frontier, overpowering the border states of the Germanic Marcomannians, the Germanic or Slavonic Quadi, the Illyreans and Gothic peoples, the supine Emperor of Constantinople had to send to him grovelling embassies. On one of these embassies was Priscus a native of Thrace. To him we are indebted for our knowledge of this savage who had entered Europe out of the Russian steppes, and who reduced to thraldom the nations whose territories his army had occupied. The Roman embassies were allowed no freedom of movement, but were met at the frontier established by Attila's armies, and then hurried, in an undignified manner, by Attila's guides along winding paths, through forests and across streams in canoes. They depended upon the local populations for supplies. It was from the people of Transylvania they received mead instead of the wine to which they were accustomed, as well as some sort of malted liquor named *camus* distilled from barley, but which bears a name very like the Tatar *koumiss*, a liquor made of fermented mare's milk.

Hungary, until much later times, was actively engaged in making mead, despite the fact that it is a wine-growing country. For we learn that one Palatinate of the Kingdom alone used to produce as much as ten thousand barrels of mead.[96]

In Lithuanian folk poetry one constantly finds references to mead :

> " To-day we will drink mead ;
> To-morrow we will march
> Into the land of the Franks." [97]
>
> .   .   .   .
>
> " To-day we'll drink ale ;
> To-morrow we'll march out
> To the land of Hungary
>
> " And what shall we drink ?
> And what shall we drink ?
> In the land of Hungary ?

" Milk, mead,
double beer,
Red wine." [98]

The last poem is of interest because it is quite clear that
the mead is ranked highly, with double beer and red wine.
In connection with Lithuania one is reminded of an account
given to the author by the Princess Radzewill, that a noble
sack-mead, with all the qualities of an Imperial Tokay, could
still be obtained there by the favoured before the Second
German War. The Princess tells me that once she obtained
a precious bottle of such mead, when travelling through the
country, and in order to disturb the lees as little as possible,
she journeyed clutching it in her arms. Later, when they
came to drink the mead, they were joined by a butterfly,
who, from fluttering around the glasses, eventually drank
from them, until a state of good cheer was replaced by downright inebriation—an intoxication of nectar which betrayed
itself in its erratic flutterings and floppings.

A folk poem of the Vod people (that tribe which lies around
Leningrad) is rather interesting. It reads :

" The beer warms you,
The brandy lights you up :
Vierland's brandy, good for drinking,
Honey-beer from our own land."

Is this a survival of the original ale ? It will be remembered that I have suggested that ale was (before malt was
used) merely a very weak mead. If gruit or hops be added
to it, it becomes a beer. We know that somewhere about
the fifteenth century hops were added to English ale, since
when it has become beer, although still called ale.

There is a possibility that honey-beer means " bracket "
(of which more later), which is a mixture of a malt- and
honey-liquor.

One old myth tells us that the Veneti (a Baltic people)
and the dwarfs lived together, and caroused at night on the
sweet mead,[99] which indicates that, at any rate, this sweet

variety of mead was certainly in use among them, as it appears still to be among the Poles.

The Mordvins, a Finnu-Ugrian people, had a beehive god and goddess, while among the Finns we have an interesting reference to the use of honey in their liquor.   In one of their magic songs, on the origin of ale, the girl, Osmotar, made

FIG. 4

An Ancient Honey-gatherer, from a prehistoric Rock painting, Arana Cave, near Bicirp, Valencia, Spain
(After R. R. Schmidt, *The Dawn of the Human Mind*)

some beer of barley and hops but she could not get it to ferment, and so she cries out :

> " What must now be added to it,
> What is needful to provide for,
> That the ale may be fermented,
> And the beer be brought to foaming ? "

Several methods were tried and failed, until Kalevatar, the lovely maiden, gave Osmotar a mustard pod, which turned into a bee, which flew off and brought back the virgin honey.

This was put into the beer, " And the beer at length fermented." [100]

There is another case [101] of a charm in which honey is brought from the isle as ferment for the ale.

It is quite clear that honey is dragged into these stories because in the folk memory it was remembered that all true liquor of old was made from the magical honey, and so a small amount of honey was still needed before the magical process of fermentation could be accomplished.

Mead, judging by their old literature, was still drunk by the Finns, despite the use of ale and beer as substitutes for it, but, as we should expect, it was reserved for special occasions, such as at the wedding feast of Ilmarinen, where we read :

> " Honey from the taps was oozing,
> Ale around the lips was foaming,
> Mead the mood of all enlivened."

E

CHAPTER V

A BRIEF ACCOUNT OF HONEY-LIQUORS OUTSIDE THE ARYAN WORLD

HONEY has not been used for the production of a wine-like liquor among the Aryans, and nearly related peoples, alone, although it is, in the form of mead, to be particularly associated with those civilizations.

It is, therefore, desirable to touch briefly upon its use among other peoples ranging from the most primitive African tribes to the pre-Columban civilizations of America, although the tradition and mythology connected with these liquors, and indeed the actual type and quality of them, will often be vastly different from that *nectar* or *soma*, the divine mead, which we have learnt was the drink of our ancestors and their gods.

Honey was no doubt the only early source of alcohol. Primitive man having robbed the wild bees' nests, and squeezed the honey from the broken and mangled combs into a pot, licked his fingers, and to avoid waste of the remaining honey in the lumps of sticky beeswax washed them in water to make therefrom a sweet drink, and to wash the wax which he used in many ways for his needs. Given right conditions, and an oversight of a week or so in consuming all his honey water in the jar, he would some day find that the insipid sweet liquor had become something which filled him with wonder and delight. Thus the making of an alcoholic liquor must have begun, among all tribes and nations everywhere. Where, of course, intensive cultivation of cereals, vines or other fruits, took place it would, as we have already seen, be early replaced in part or whole by beer, wine, and fruit-wines, since these are normally a more prolific source of alcohol than is honey. As a consequence, in such countries mead would not reach as high a state of perfection, as where it remained the principal liquor, as it did among the Aryans. However, it does not follow that outside of the wine- and beer-drinking countries the making of mead would necessarily reach high levels. This would no doubt depend upon the state of civilization enjoyed by the peoples concerned. We cannot speak for the quality of pre-Columban mead in America, but, among peoples already reaching a fair measure of civilization, we may at least give it the benefit of the doubt, and assume that it was something more than a mere alcoholic liquor. Elsewhere, such forms of honey-drink as have been made, and are still made, are primitive in keeping with the state of culture of the tribes which drink them, and so not to be confused with that liquor which the Aryans prized so highly. For this reason it is doubtful if they should be called meads, since the intention of the makers of these liquors is merely to exploit the sugars in the honey for the alcohol which can be made from it. Flavour and bouquet no doubt are matters of little importance, and the liquor is drunk new. Furthermore, the adulterants added, and the method of manufacture, really turn the liquor into a form of a honey-beer. These liquors are, therefore, no more mead than the palm-toddy they drink is wine.

However, for the sake of completeness, we will briefly discuss these liquors which in some measure are related to mead.

The Australian native is among the most primitive in the world, yet he has an intoxicating drink, which, it has been said, according to Hilda M. Ransome, has been reported by one traveller in New South Wales as having been made from honey.[102]

In Africa we find that there are several wines and beers drunk by the native peoples. All over the Continent are found millet beer, for instance, drunk by the A-Zande of the Anglo-Egyptian Sudan:[103] the Waduruma[104] and the Bantu[105] use a palm-wine; the Kikuyu and Kamba tribes of East Africa drink both sugar-cane as well as a

honey-beer.[106] These tribes probably have other liquors
as well.

Besides the Kikuyu and Kamba tribes drinking a honey-
beer, we also find it among the Dorōbo of Kenya,[107] the
Ba-Kaonda of Northern Rhodesia [108] and the Masai.[109]

This honey-liquor is evidently a beer or something very
like a beer in strength. It is always called a beer by social
anthropologists, and that term is justified where the liquor
is flavoured with herbs or adulterants. On the other hand
it is clear that in some cases where none are added the term
ale would be more correct. Indeed, in some of these cases,
what we have still being made among the primitive tribes of
Africa is something not unrelated to that original form of
ale which was common also to our own Aryan forebears—a
very weak mead, of no body, and consequently no keeping
powers, intended to be drunk immediately after making.

Certainly the liquor described in the following song of the
Kikuyu would appear to be *ale* and not *beer*—

> " In due season we hang a beehive on a tree.
> Then father goes up and takes the honey.
> He climbs up with a bag and puts the honey in it.
> He calls his wife who mixes the honey with water.
> The husband asks his wife,
> Is the honey [' ale '] ready to drink ?
> They spend the whole day drinking the ' ale '.
> The whole company becomes overcome with liquor." [110]

These African peoples appear to drink the liquor in the
earliest stages of fermentation, for not only is it inferred that
the liquor is newly made in the above song, but we are told
expressly that among the Masai it takes only six days to
make.[111]

Therefore it is quite clear that this liquor is not to be
compared with mead, a liquor of wine strength, and, among
advanced peoples, of age and growth.

Nevertheless, poor as such liquors are compared with
genuine mead, because they share the superiority of mead
over other liquors made from cheaper raw materials, it is not

surprising that even these primitive peoples set a mark upon them.

This is seen in the fact that among the Kamba tribes the honey-beer (? or -ale) is poured out as a libation to the ancestral spirits ; [112] while, among the Masai and Kikuyu tribes, it is reserved on most occasions for the leaders of the people, and on some occasions it may only be drunk by the elders and no one else.[113] The Masai also use it for sprinkling, in a ritual of blessing the warriors by the elders.[114]

It is to be expected owing to the nature of honey and mead (or in this case honey-ale) that some of the myths which have arisen among these primitive peoples connected with them should have certain things in common with ideas held by the Aryan and adjacent civilizations. But, on the whole, the cases where there are ideas in common are remarkably few. While, on the contrary, there are myths and practices among these coloured peoples which make it quite clear that in certain essentials there is nothing in common between their heritage and our own. For instance, there is not merely no equivalent of our *honeymoon* tradition, with its feasts of mead, but the very opposite. For instance the Thonga people of South Africa severely restrict the use of honey for a year after marriage ! [115]

Despite the plentifulness of the vine in America we find that a honey-liquor was drunk in pre-Columban days. No doubt, as elsewhere, this was the special liquor ; for lesser folk, or lesser occasions, other liquors would be drunk. Some indication of what these might have been is afforded by the surviving liquors recorded as being drunk in Central America. The native peoples of Mexico for instance drink *pulque*, which is prepared from the fermented juice of the agave (or American aloe) and is a heavy flavoured liquor, resembling sour milk, but prized by the natives. It is a liquor which is ready in less than a fortnight for drinking, and so one of no character.[116] This liquor is prepared relatively hygienically, although the juice is first sucked out of the plant ! But the natives of Guiana, of whose liquor

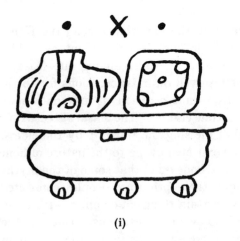

(i)

(ii)

FIG. 5

Maya Hieroglyphs for—(i) Honey and Honey Jar;
(ii) Mead Jar

(After Ransome, *The Sacred Bee*)

Sir Everard Im Thurn wrote [117] produce their *paiware* in what is probably the most disgusting manner of any alcoholic liquor, although the ordinary run of it is apparently quite pleasant to the taste. The natives chew the cassava bread, which is then mixed with water, and allowed a short period of fermentation !

The Mayas, who were a civilized people living in the Bronze age when the Spaniards conquered them, had a mead, or rather a metheglin of some sort. It was evidently prepared from honey and water and flavoured with some herb. As the *glyph* or sign on the Maya pictographs representing mead is the one *cib*, and since *ci* represents the *pulque* made from the American aloe (also called agave or maguey plant) already described, it is probable that the honey-liquor was flavoured with this plant. In which case *pulque* as now made by the Mexican natives is a degenerate of the honey-liquor of their more civilized ancestors.[118] What the quality of this liquor was we do not know. If *pulque* is anything to go by it would suggest it was rather a honey-beer than a true metheglin.

It was, however, considered of some importance in the life of the Maya since it had a god to itself—*Acan*. The gods of the four quarters of the world, the four *Bacabs* as they were called, were also the harvest and food gods, and consequently were known as *Acantum*. Thus these *Bacabs* were also gods of mead.[119]

The health-giving qualities of mead were, apparently, recognized by the Maya, but so far as we can tell there does not seem to be any sacred association connected with it as we find among the Aryans.[120] Indeed, that belief seems to be peculiar to our own ancestors, and where it is found elsewhere among neighbouring peoples, it was probably derived from them.

The North American Indians appear to have had no wines of any sort, or at least very little use for them. Across the Pacific their fellow Mongoloid races, the Chinese and Japanese, do not appear to have been so comfortless, but even so the use of wines and beers seems to have been far less common than it is with either the white or the black races.   China, for instance, has native vines, and yet it has no indigenous wine industry.   Palm wine is made to some extent, and spirits are made from rice, while, even more disgusting than the natives of Guiana, spirits are produced from putrefied meat of mares and ewe-lambs ! [121]   Of mead there is scarcely a trace, as might be expected among a people, no matter how civilized they may have been in other directions, who were so barbarous in their liquors.   There is a word for mead evidently borrowed from the Aryans, and wherever and whenever it may have been made in China it must be accounted of Aryan origin.   An exception among Mongoloid peoples is perhaps to be found in the Korean who have, at any rate, a mead-brandy of some sort called *misshu.*

It is an equally curious thing to reflect that among the related Tatar and other Mongol peoples further west, neither honey nor grape forms a part of their beverages.   That the vine does not is perhaps to be expected, as they are migratory peoples.   But this does not account for the lack of mead. On the other hand, like the Chinese, but less disgustingly so, they turn to the animal for their alcohol, and make it from fermented milk—*koumiss.*

Except for the pre-Columban peoples of central and southern America, it would seem that on the whole a knowledge and taste for mead, and even for wine, seems to have been little developed throughout the whole Mongoloid group of races, and even where in ancient times there would seem to have been some slight knowledge of it, as in China, it has long passed out of knowledge, in the case of mead, and almost so in the case of wine.

It may be that among the Mongoloids there is a lessened desire for wines than among the white and black races. Their religions tend to frown severely upon alcohol, but this is hardly likely to be the cause of its rather restricted use, and more likely to be the result of a natural inclination. Furthermore, such tendencies might be reinforced by the large use of narcotics among wide sections of this race. For instance, although the American Indians did not drink wines or ales they smoked tobacco, and the Chinese have been addicted to opium, which they use in much the same way as alcohol is employed, as a stimulant. It is said that when the opium-smoker has plenty of active work to do, opium " appears to be no more injurious than smoking tobacco ".[122] It is, of course, also among these peoples that the drinking and widespread use of tea at an early date occurred, and it would seem hard to escape the conclusion that probably tobacco- and opium-smoking, combined with tea-drinking, go a long way towards making the need for the finer liquors like mead and wine unnecessary.

There is some ground for thinking that this may be the case, in view of the fact that the ever-increasing consumption of tobacco and tea among ourselves is progressively characterized by a fall in the consumption of wine. Furthermore, it would seem to change the popular demands in wine. The palate of the smoker is coarsened, although he will rarely admit it, and this must lead him to demand stronger and more pungent liquors to drink. Consequently the change (where not influenced by political or economic considerations) from pure wine-drinking to a love of highly alcoholized wines, and naked spirits, must in part be associated with the demand for tobacco, and presumably, where it occurs, for other narcotics such as opium.

Certainly the experience of Moslem countries would appear to support the view that man must have some form of exhilaration and if he does not derive it from alcohol he turns to narcotics, and these, on the whole, are in opposition to one another, and where the narcotics take a hold they seem to have a tighter grip and drive out liquor. In *The Thousand and One Nights*, a collection of tales written down before the introduction of tobacco in the seventeenth century, and which present a faithful account of Arabic life, we find that wine was commonly drunk. But now among most Arabic nations, tobacco and coffee have everywhere driven out wine, aided and abetted as they are by widespread consumption of hemp, as hasheesh, and by opium, these latter not being merely smoked but consumed in other ways, as conserves.[123]

However, be all this as it may. The fact remains that our meads and liquors partly or wholly compounded from honey, would appear to be mainly restricted to the white and black races, with certain notable exceptions, such as among the civilized pre-Columban peoples of America. But it is only among the white peoples, and particularly among the Aryans, that mead reached such a great degree of development that it was considered to be all these things—the sacred liquor of the gods, the bestower of health and strength, wit and poetry, and to have the power of reproduction and of immortality. Nowhere else do we find this *nectar, ambrosia* or *soma*.

CHAPTER VI

THE ARRIVAL OF GRUIT AND STRONG-DRINK:
BEER AND CIDER

BEFORE we can proceed with the study of the history of our mead we must turn aside to touch upon the arrival of beer, for it will have been observed that we have been careful so far to speak of ale only in relation to mead, and have failed to give explanations of the references made to beer in some of the quotations.

It might be asked why this stress upon the words beer and ale when both drinks are so much alike. There are reasons why we must keep them apart—no matter how much the modern products under those names by reason of their present-day similarity may have caused confusion.

We have already seen that ale was a form of light mead, originally being made from honey. Later, when the knowledge of malting spread from the ancient, warm, temperate world to the north, the use of malted barley (as a cheap substitute) took the place of honey. But in character it was still far different from beer—lacking both the strength as well as the bitterness of beer, which to-day we derive from hops. Evidence of this latter distinction between beer and ale is clear. For we have in 1483 a petition from the ale-brewers to the Lord Mayor of London asking him to forbid the putting into the ale of any " hops, herbs or any other like thing, but only licor, malte and yeste ". Thus, up to the end of the fifteenth century, it was recognized that ale was a drink made solely from malt, as the original ale had been made from honey.

Further, another reason why we must keep the two names apart is that the Anglo-Saxons and Norsemen themselves at the dawn of history make a distinction, and since we know that there evidently was an inherent difference (the addition of bitter herbs or hops in making beer and the greater strength of beer over ale), we must not confuse these liquors.

How the knowledge of beer-making reached the north we do not know. It might have been quite early, brought by men of the Atlantic race who built the megalithic monuments. We have already seen that Babylonia and Egypt were both beer-drinking countries and it has been suggested that they gave to the north (as well as to prehistoric Spain and France) the idea of malting barley as a substitute for honey. Whether they gave the Aryans the trick of making a bitter drink so early as prehistoric times is not known. But it is sufficient to say that whereas ale is an Aryan drink like mead, beer belongs to the Sumerian-Hamitic world, no matter how long it may have been with us an accepted drink.

Nevertheless, the art of beer-making was well established at the beginning of northern history.

We find, for example, that in Anglo-Saxon the word for a feast or banquet is a " beer-drinking " [124] a " booze " in other words. [125]

It is therefore somewhat strange to our modern eyes to read such passages as St. Luke, 5, 29 and 9, 14 :

" *And Lēvi dyde him mycelne gebēorscype on his hūse.*"
" And Levi made him a great feast (beer-drinking) in his own house."
" *Dā cwaeþ hē to his leorningcnihtum,   Doþ þaet hig sitton, þurh*
" And he said to his disciples,   Make them sit down by
gebeorscypas f ȳ ftegum."
fifties in a company." [126]

In the same gospel we have the Latin Vulgate word *sicera* translated by *beor*, beer. The word *sicera* is from the Greek σικερα, meaning " strong drink, and a sweet fermented liquor " and it is related to the Hebrew *Shâkar*, " to be intoxicated ". [127]

It is clear from the remark of Pliny, [128] who comments on the fact that the western nations did not water their beer as wine is watered, that the western, Mediterranean and Near Eastern beer must have had a consistency and strength comparable with wine to occasion such a remark. The only beer to-day which would be comparable would be the various college beers and audits, which are wines rather than beers. This use of the word *beer* for *sicera* would seem to suggest that beer, in contrast with ale, was originally a strong audit type of beer. If so this would suggest its relationship originally to the beer referred to by Pliny.

Therefore the fall of beer from the position of a " strong-drink " to just *beer* must have occurred (if this theory is correct) between the time the surviving gospels were translated (at the end of the tenth century) and the Middle Ages. If this theory is incorrect—and early Anglo-Saxon beer was not unduly strong—then the expression " strong-drink " could only refer to the taste, and, if so, that would be attributable to the herbs with which it was flavoured in contrast to the unflavoured ale. Thi salternative theory, however, presents a difficulty, because no such similar solution can be called for in the case of cider—and obviously one is required since cider is a corruption of *sicera*, and so, also, must have been a strong drink in the beginning.

Besides the reference to beer in the Anglo-Saxon Bible we have frequent references to it in *Beowulf*. For instance, we read of beer and beer-drinking and of the hall being called the beer-hall, of beer being served in a flagon, and so on.[129]

The fact that the word *beer* could connote a feast and give its name to the drinking-hall seems to suggest that, after *mead*, beer was looked upon as a noble drink. Therefore all the evidence goes to support a strong, rich brew as the type of our old English beer in the time of the Venerable Bede or of Beowulf. In partial support of this interpretation must be borne in mind the fact that in the Middle Ages beer was still stronger than ale. Thus, in the fourteenth century " better " beer could be got at 4*d.* a gallon, whereas ale went down to as low as 1*d.* (" penny " ale). This may have been the survival of the tradition of beer as a " strong-drink ". Furthermore, in added support of this originally much greater strength of beer, is the fact that according to Bateson's

Mediaeval England when Dover was provisioned in the Middle Ages 260 quarters of malt were required to brew 520 gallons of beer. This means we have here a very strong beer. Probably the origin of the weak modern beer lies in the " small " beers which were produced by second washings of the mash prepared for these strong beers. These " small " beers appear later to have been called " ales " as well as " small " beers.

But putting aside, however, this difference of strength as a distinction between ale and beer, and putting aside the inherent difference of origin—ale being but a weakened mead and then later a weak mead-like drink in which malt has been substituted for honey, whereas beer is a malt liquor from the beginning—we have one further difference, and this difference is all important. Beer was a drink in which bitter herbs had been infused to give a strong and bitter taste. Whereas mead, and the original ale, depended on the essences of the honey for flavour, and later ale for the flavours it drew from the malt.

In England and northern Europe these bitter herbs were known as *gruit*. Everyone had different formulas for making the gruit and many of the religious houses had monopolies in the gruit trade. This mixture often consisted of such as sweet gale or bog myrtle, marsh or wild rosemary, milfoil or yarrow and other ingredients. The herbs were chosen not only for their flavour but often for medicinal reasons, as was the case in the original manufacture of the formulas of many liqueurs, since there was a constant search for elixirs of life. Such as borage was in great repute for these purposes and we find John Evelyn in his *Acetaria* echoes these ideas when he tells us that it should be used in wine to revive the hypo-chondriac and cheer the hard student. We find Salmon's *Household Companion* (1710) recording it as one of the four cordial flowers, because it comforted the heart, cheered melancholy, and revived the fainting spirits. Balm, another herb in great demand, was used for the digestion and to " expel the melancholy vapours ". But whatever the mixtures, they were as jealously guarded as are, to-day, the formulas used in the production of many of the famous liqueurs.

A survival of such beer made with a gruit of sorts seems to have existed near Litchfield in the seventeenth century,[130] where ling was the herb added, and until the present century a kind of beer made with a " groot " continued to be made in the South Hams of Devon.

With the discovery of hops we have a case once more of the substitute. With its very strong astrigent flavour hops will go further than much more of gruit in infusing its flavour in a brew. The result is it was much cheaper, and so, just as the cheaper malt pushed out honey in ale-making, so the use of gruit in beer was threatened and ultimately replaced by hops. Therefore, not only has beer changed its character considerably so far as strength is concerned, but also by the use of this one bitter herb in place of mixtures of many other and more subtle herbs.

Gruit was not replaced by its cheaper substitute without a struggle, for it had powerful supporters. The monasteries, and other great interests, often had monopolies and they fought to retain the use of gruit. It is worth noting, in passing, that not only had the monasteries great interest in the growing of the herbal gruit but also in beer-making until the twelfth and thirteenth centuries. Gradually this trade passed more and more into the hands of the laity, and so a brewers' corporation grew up, as the Guild of Our Lady and St. Thomas à Becket. Because of the Church's interest in brewing we find that Archbishop Frederick of Cologne in 1381 issued on behalf of the gruit monopoly a decree requiring all (clergy, civilians and military, as well as the brewers) to buy their gruit in the episcopal gruit-houses. At the same time the importation of hopped beer from Westphalia was forbidden.[131]

But, if we may judge by a petition to the Lord Mayor and Aldermen of the City of London in 1464 the use of hops in brewing had come into established practice by that time.

By the sixteenth century hops were used not only in beer but in ale (despite the petition, to which earlier reference has been made, of the ale-brewers to the Lord Mayor to forbid the putting of either gruit or hops into ale).   In other words, ale ceased to be brewed, and has not been brewed in England since, and it is a complete misnomer to call certain varieties of beer *ale*.[132]

Therefore, when we drink modern " ale " we are not drinking the same drink to which Chaucer refers in the *Monk's Prologue*.

> " Our hoste seyde, as I am faithful man,
>   And by the precious corpus Madrian,
>   I hadde lever than a barel ale
>   That goode lief my wyf hadde herd this tale." [133]

But while the true (unhopped) ale had ceased to be brewed in England by the sixteenth century, it was, apparently, still to be found in Scotland.   For we read of a Jerome Cardan, a French physician, who travelled in Scotland on a visit to Archbishop Hamilton in 1552.   He frequently mentions food, which appears to have had an attraction for him, and he approves of Scotch ale—*hala* as he calls it.   It reminded him of " sweet white-mist ", and he says that " it differs from beer in the omission of the hops ".

From which it would seem that we have lost something worth while in the disappearance of the older form of ale and its replacement by beer.[134]

Although in its origins quite unrelated to ale or beer, this is the place in which it is convenient to refer to cider, since the Anglo-Saxons regarded not only beer as a " strong drink " but also cider.

We have seen that the word *beor* is used to translate the Latin Vulgate word *sicera* meaning " strong drink " in the Anglo-Saxon gospels.   An opposite process has occurred in the case of cider.   The Latin word *sicera* itself was adopted into English, and, strange as it may seem, cider is the very word, *sicera*, meaning a " strong drink ".[135]   Wyclif spells cider as sither, cyther, sidir and syder. Chaucer has ciser, siser, sythir and cyder.

Thus we find that in the story of Sampson where in the Bible it says that he drank neither " strong drink " nor wine, Chaucer in his *Monk's Tale* [136] says : " This Sampson never ciser drank, ne wyn."

It is interesting to find that *sisere* was the form still in use in the Channel Islands as late as the eighteenth century.[137]

It is quite clear that there were two ways of rendering " *sicera* " into English. Either as " beer ", using an English word for a strong liquor made of malt and bitter herbs, or else by anglicizing the word *sicera* and using it for an equally strong native apple (or even pear) drink. At first, no doubt, there was some confusion in the use of the word *sicera*, and this is surely reflected in the fact that the Abbot of Burton's very fine beer was sometimes called cicer, somewhere about 1295.[138]

Nevertheless, it is certain that among the early English there were two really strong liquors, cider and beer. Ale was a light drink, while mead, in common with wine generally, could range from a strong drink to a lighter, according to its particular type, but of this more anon.

That ancient cider was a strong apple (and if need be pear) wine, is clear from another piece of evidence. The Manichaeans accused Catholic Europe of being much given to wine-drinking, a habit of which they said they were free. But, in reply, St. Augustine replied that while it was true that these Manichaeans did not drink wine, they nevertheless drank apple-juice, which was more delicious than all other wines. While Tartullian tells us that cider was most strong and vinous. (*Succum ex pomis vinosissimum.*)

It must come as a great surprise to most people to realize that this drink (the proprietary brands of which are now drunk by those who consider our already weakened beer too strong) was once, like *ancient* beer itself, a forceful liquor. Of course it still can be when bought from the farms in England or Normandy, but I venture to think that even these

F

farm ciders themselves are merely the survival of the weaker vintages of old days, because (besides my own) I once tasted a cider, and several bottles of it too, at Halesworth, which was as strong as good sherry.[139]   This cider had been made and bottled in the house and kept several years—and it was a prince of wines despite being a little too sweet.   Here indeed is surely the only cider that could justify being called a strong drink—*sicera*.   As a weaker cider is now the recognized type of apple-liquor it is advisable to use one of the earlier forms of the word (such as cyser, siser, or sicera) to denote the genuine strong apple wine, made, as it was, with honey, and therefore, as a consequence, a kind of sack-mead.

We are told, by one writer on the subject, that cider was first made in England in 1284,[140] but, as we have already seen, it was served by Harold Godwinson, at a royal banquet, two centuries earlier.   Furthermore, as the apple was known and used throughout the Aryan world, it is inconceivable that so late a period should see either the discovery of this drink or its introduction into Britain.   As Sir George Birdwood [141] has said, the apple is the natural wine tree for the northern Aryans (long before their break-up into Slavs, Goths and Celts) as the date palm is for the Babylonian or the vine for the Greeks and Romans.

The fact is, however, that cider is not often mentioned by the Anglo-Saxons and it is late in appearing in literature. It may not be without significance that although the word " apple " belongs to the Anglo-Saxon language in common with other Aryan languages it is usually found in place-names coupled with Celtic roots, such as in the names Appledore, Appledurcombe, and in Avalon, or, on the other hand, it is found in Norse names, such as Appleby, Applegarth and Applethwaite.[142]

Of equal significance may be the fact that the greater number of the chief areas of apple-growing and cider-making lie in the West of England, bordering upon the Celtic regions, and in northern France and the Channel Islands, where the Norsemen settled.

From all these facts it is probable that an extensive cultivation of apples did not take place among the Anglo-Saxons, and therefore cider would be little known or used compared with ale or mead. The Norsemen (we may assume), on the other hand, used the apple more extensively. But the only Norse territory suitable to apple (and so cider) production was Normandy.

In that case the production of cider was probably introduced late to the English either from the Celts, Norsemen or Normans. If this is so, we may have the explanation of how " ciser " (from which we get the word cider) came to replace beer as the translation of *sicera*, and why we have no native name for the apple-wine.

We have shown that beer must have been a strong drink in the tenth century and it has been suggested that it would be of an " audit " character. But by the fourteenth century (although stronger than ale) it had become quite a weak drink, not much stronger than at present. It was therefore somewhere between the tenth and the fourteenth centuries that it had clearly become necessary for some other word than beer to be used to translate the Biblical *sicera* or strong drink. That would account for a new liquor of a strong character becoming known by the anglicized form of the foreign word *sicera* owing to the absence of a real English word for the new strong drink. If these hypotheses are correct then it would seem that early cider was like the Halesworth type—a really strong vintage, well able to represent the strong palm-toddy which the Bible calls in the Vulgate version *Sicera*. The fifteenth century quotation that " without sidir and wijn and meeth men and wommen my3te lyve full long " [143] confirms this. No one to-day could think either of coupling mead, wine and cider together, or would imagine that the modern variant of cider could ever contain sufficient alcohol to shorten anyone's life.

The decline of beer as a strong drink, and its approximation to ale in strength, was probably due to the Norman conquest which introduced a wine-drinking people. The artisan and peasant classes could scarcely have afforded an audit type of beer for common use and as the Norman gentry and burghers who set the fashion no longer patronized it in its old form, because of their taste for wine, the beer was bound to become less of a wine-like drink and more of an ale.

But cider itself has undergone the same degeneration in the course of time and no longer is a strong drink.   This is probably due to the influence of sack, hippocras and pyment which became fashionable in the Middle Ages, and later, and which supplied the need for a strong dessert wine.

This degeneration was of course progressive, and not likely to occur rapidly.   Consequently if we go back to the time of James I we discover that it was still very much stronger than it is to-day.   For we find it referred to, with perry, which would have much the same qualities, in association with metheglin and strong ale, and expressly called a heavy liquor, in the ballad called " The Man in the Moon Drinks Claret " :

> " O my noddle too heavy doth way !
> Metheglin, perry, syder nor strong ale,
> Are half so hevy, be they nere so stale." [144]

Thus, it is quite evident, that although we may accept to-day these weak drinks as beer and cider, they are not what our ancestors believed to be *beor* and *cyser*.   And so when we drink a college beer, or a special cider like the Halesworth type, or the cysers once more being revived, we are actually partaking of the old-fashioned drinks which bore those names. These, and these alone are the genuine articles.

Before leaving the discussion of beer it is of interest to mention a theory suggested by Hilda M. Ransome [145] who says that there is a close connection between *biuza*, an old word for beer, and the Saxon word for bee which is *beo*. Thus, she goes on to say—" Perhaps these may both have meant honey . . . and biuza may be a composite word for *bi-wesa* or *bi-wisa*, which really denoted honey or bee-juice."

It is of interest to note the fact that the word *barley* is derived from *beer*, since, in later times, however it was first made, beer came to be made from barley. The ancient name for barley survived in the Anglo-Saxon name for August, which was called the *Gerst* month. Had *ancient* beer been made from barley and not from honey we should expect some relationship between the early word for the raw material and the liquor.

If these views are correct, it would suggest that the incoming strong, malted and bitter liquor from the Mediterranean was a substitute for some strong mead liquor of the ancient Anglo-Saxons before the dawn of history : and in that case, it may be that " *biuza* " or " beer " was indeed an old word for that strong mead drink which to-day is nameless, unless we call it " *strong* " mead or, as has been done in this book, following established precedents, " *sack* "-mead. The fact that we have no old native name for sack-mead, which is such a distinctive mead, is very significant. It is certain that in olden times " beer " (*biuza* as it probably was originally) was held in such high esteem that it competes throughout with mead in giving its name to the hall where the household sat long over their drink in the evenings. If all this is so, then not only have we the case of the light mead, which was anciently called " ale ", being replaced by a malt substitute, but also the strong sack-mead, being, in part, ousted by another substitute, compounded of a strong brew of malt and bitter herbs.

By historic times in the north of Europe there is little doubt that " beer " was a strong malt liquor. Yet, it would seem that there must have lingered on in the minds of many, at any rate, the knowledge that originally " beer " had been a mead drink, since we find the Anglo-Saxon word *beor* being used to translate *hydromeli* (mead), *mel* (honey) and *mulsum* (which as we shall see later is compounded of honey).

Following this line of thought, it would seem highly probable that somewhere before the dawn of north European history, not only were three varieties of mead made (which in the nature of things would be natural enough), but civilization had advanced so far that they were definitely classified, as *biuza* (sack-mead), mead, and ale (light mead) ; and it was only with the development of malt substitutes for the more costly honey that confusion set in, so far as the original nature of *biuza* and ale were concerned.   In time, this led to the word *beer* (a later word than *biuza*) being transferred to *gerst* (barley) from which the substitute for honey-*biuza* or -beer had come to be made.   This accounts for barley, a word which would appear to be connected with honey, being used for a cereal from which malt is made.

CHAPTER VII

MEAD IN THE MIDDLE AGES AND TILL THE EIGHTEENTH CENTURY

TO turn back to mead, which we have outrun in our attempt to trace the development of these other liquors with whose history it is interlocked, the Middle Ages did not see the disappearance of mead, or a decline in the estimation in which it was held. For instance, at Munich, in Bavaria, great quantities of mead were drunk. Ulm in the twelfth century was a celebrated mead-making town, while the Baltic towns of Riga and Danzig were equally well known for its production. Indeed there was sufficient mead made at these times, that on one occasion, at Meissen in Saxony, in 1015, it was used to put out a fire as the inhabitants had no water ! Whilst, at Eger in Bohemia, in 1460, there were no fewer than thirteen mead-houses, producing as much as 384 barrels a year. But after the Reformation, and at the end of the Thirty Years' War, in 1684, there was only one such house left in this town. I am informed that Hitchin in Hertfordshire was also noted for its mead-houses.

There can be little doubt that in the time of Chaucer it was still placed in the front rank in England, as we can see from several references which he makes to it. For instance, in the *Knight's Tale* [146] he has mead used as the wine for sacrifice :

> " His maydens, that she thider with hire ledde,
> Full redily with them the fyr they hadde,
> Thencens, the clothés, and the remnant al
> That to the sacrificé longen shall,
> The hornés fulle of meeth, as was the gyse,—
> There lakkéd noght to doon hir sacrifise."

Again in the *Tale of Sir Thopas* [147] we read :

> " ' Do come,' he seyde, ' my mynstrales,
> And geestours for to tellen tales,
> Anon in my armýnge ;

Of romances that been roiales,
Of Popès and of Cardinales,
And eek of love-likynge.'

They set hym first the sweete **wyn**
And mede eek in a mazelyn,
And roial spicerye ;
And gynger breed that was full **fyn,**
And lycorys, and eek comyn,
With sugre that is so trye."

In the *Miller's Tale* [148] Chaucer tells of a merry priest
of a not strictly priestly character who, in rivalry of a
clerk, sought the favours of a beautiful housewife of his town.
In the course of this wooing Parson Absolon showers upon the
lady all the best he can buy.   And, because she was a townswoman and therefore presumably of more delicate taste and
nurture than a countrywoman was supposed to be, he sent
her meeth (mead), pyment and other delicacies :

" Fro day to day this joly Absolon
So woweth hire that hym is won begon ;
He waketh all the night and al the day,
He kembeth his lokkès brode and made hym gay,
He woweth her by meenés and brocage,
And swoor he woldé been hire owene page ;
He syngeth, brokkynge as a nyghtyngale ;
He sente hire pyment, *meeth*, and spiced ale,
And wafres, pipyng hoot out of the gleede,
And, for she was of towne, he profreth meede ;
For some folk wol ben wonnen for richesse,
And somme for strokes, and somme for gentillesse."

In Germany, in the Middle Ages, we read of the Judges
being served with mead—which speaks for itself since the
bar has always been distinguished for its discrimination in
these matters.   The army too would appear to have appreciated the qualities of mead for we find that in 1390, for Earl
Derby's Expedition, there was provided " xxiiij barellis de
meed ".

In 1460, we find the sack-mead being used by one writer
as a standard of sweetness—" It is sweeter then med ".[149]

Somewhere after the Middle Ages we begin to read of

metheglin, which was a mead drink.   It is to be found, for instance, in Shakespeare.[150]

Berowne : White-handed mistress, one sweet word with thee.
Princess : Honey, and milk, and sugar ; there is three.
Berowne : Nay then, two treys, and if you grow so nice,
            Metheglin, wort, and malmsey : well run, dice !
            There's half-a-dozen sweets.

     .   .   .   .

Page : And as poor as Job ?
Ford : And as wicked as his wife ?
Evans : And given to fornications, and to taverns, and sack and wine and metheglins, and to drinkings and swearings and starings, pribbles and prabbles.

This word metheglin is a Welsh word, and it is the angliciza-tion of *Meddyglyn*, meaning a spiced mead.[151]

It would seem that the Welsh favoured a spiced mead to any other type, not merely from the fact that they have given their name generally to this variety of the liquor, but also from the literary evidence at our disposal.   Thus we read, for instance, in one sixteenth-century writer [152]—" Metheglyn, which is moste used in Wales, by reason of hotte herbes boyled with honey, is hotter than meade " ; and again in a seven-teenth-century work [153]—" Some metheglings, the wine of Wales."

Whereas mead can and does range from a dinner wine to a dessert (sack-mead), metheglin would seem to have been always a sack or sweet drink.   Thus we read in the seven-teenth-century Butler—" Methæglen is the more generous or stronger Hydromel, being unto Mede as Vinum to Lora." [154]

The type of herbs used in metheglin are given in the seventeenth-century Venner in the following recipe as—" If Rosemary, Hyssop, Time, Orgaine, and Sage, be first well boyled in the water, whereof you make the Metheglin, it will be the better." [155]

It is probable that metheglin spread into England gradually from the west and its use by Shakespeare was possibly derived from his native Warwickshire, which lies over against the borders of Wales.   To-day the word metheglin, used for any

kind of mead, is found well-established as far west as Oxford-
shire and Berkshire, and as far south as the Hampshire
borders of Berkshire, where Gilbert White, in his *Natural
History*, records it.   But in eastern England, and in most of
Wessex, the simpler and less cumbersome word mead still
reigns uncontaminated by this Welsh intruder.   The Tudors,
a Welsh dynasty, probably aided the spread of the word in
English society, for the period was one of quite debased
wine-drinking tastes, when sweet spicy wines were greatly in
demand.   They even burnt their sack to give it a flavour and
then, sweet wine as it was, actually added sugar to it !   We
are fortunate in possessing Queen Elizabeth's own royal recipe
for her mead, which is clearly a metheglin, being spiced with
rosemary, bay-leaves, sweet briar and thyme.   Under such
influence, both of popular taste, and royal favour, spiced
sack-mead (metheglin) must have become a favourite liquor.

Therefore, while up to the Middle Ages we may assume
with some degree of certainty that mead was *mead*, and not
spiced mead, and that metheglin must have been spiced mead
only, by Tudor times these terms had lost their precise
meaning, metheglin tending to be used at Court and in the
Western Midlands (as it is to-day) as a generalized term for
any type of mead although meaning particularly spiced mead,
and mead, while probably still referring in the main to true
mead, owing to a vulgar imitation of the courtly drink, was
gradually becoming a metheglin.

The result of this is to-day that where the art of mead-
making has survived in country house or with the old-
fashioned bee-master, it is mainly spiced mead, based on the
debased recipes of Tudor England, which is made, whether
it is called mead or metheglin.   But even where proper mead
may be made, it would be as like as not called metheglin
anywhere west of Berkshire.

Nevertheless, these two words ought not to be so confused,
and metheglin should only be used for spiced mead.   Metheglin among meads is what vermouths are among wines.
All vermouths are wines but all wine is not vermouth, and,

likewise, all metheglins are meads, but all mead is not metheglin.

Mead, whether as the true mead, or as metheglin, continued to enjoy the support of patrons in the succeeding Stuart times, although, for reasons which will be gone into later, the Reformation had seen a sudden shrinkage in its production, so that it was becoming a less common drink among the people as a whole.

Thus we can read in Barclay's *Argenis* (1, XVIII, 49), 1625,—" By occasion of their mead they fell unto talke of bees." While one of the most graceful compliments was paid to mead in Stuart times by Howell, Clerk to the Privy Council, in 1640, who wrote :

> " The juice of Bees, not Bacchus, here behold,
> Which British Bards were wont to quaff of old ;
> The berries of the grape with Furies swell,
> But in the honeycomb the Graces dwell."

Samuel Pepys was an enquiring person who was ever on the look out for the good things of this life, and, therefore, it is not surprising to read of his telling how he came to gain access to Charles II's own dinner, and drank his metheglin, of which Pepys speaks with praise.[156]

" At White Hall : we find the Court gone to Chapel, it being St. James's day. And by and by, while they are at Chapel . . . people came out of the Park telling us that the guns are heard plainly. And so everybodye to the Park . . . and the King and the Duke into the bowling-green, and upon the leads, whither I went and there the guns were plain to be heard. . . . By and by the King to dine, and I waited there his dining. . . . Here I met Mr. Williams who would have me to dine where he was invited to dine, at the Backestayres. So after the King's meat was taken away, we thither . . . where we dined with meat that came from his (the King's) table ; which was most excellent, with most brave drink cooled in ice (which at this hot time was welcome), and I drinking no wine had metheglin for the King's own drinking which did please me mightily."

According to Sir Kenelm Digby a certain Master Webbe was the King's own mead-maker, for we read under his account of Master Webbe's recipe—" Master Webbe, who

maketh the Kings Meathe, ordereth it thus," and so on.   The
recipe is of interest as it confirms what we would suspect from
Pepys' reference to the icing of this mead, that it was more
of a table than a dessert wine.   It was just within the dry
group, and of a full alcoholic strength for a natural wine.
Such a liquor would be improved by cooling, indeed mead is
at its best when so treated, but a sweeter sack-mead would
not respond to that treatment—and certainly not the sweet
syrupy sack-meads of Queen Elizabeth.

Although mead was very much in decline, as has been
observed, it was still treasured in the great houses, and among
the discerning, as is seen from the remarkable book of Sir
Kenelm Digby, entitled—*The Closet of the Eminently Learned
Sir Kenelme Digbie Kt. Opened : Whereby is Discovered Several
ways for making of Metheglin, Sider, Cherry-Wine . . . London,
1669.*   Sir Kenelm Digby was one of the foremost courtiers
of his day, a great amateur, who turned his attention from
naval raiding to philosophy and religion, and from that to
embassage and scientific discovery, and who, like all great
men of learning and culture, did not believe that it demeaned
his dignity to busy himself with mead-house, brewery, still-
room or kitchen—hence his *Closet Opened.*   In this we have
106 recipes for mead, which he calls indifferently mead,
metheglin, and hydromel, although strictly speaking they are
all metheglins—that is spiced meads.   By this time it is clear
that the influence of brewing had completely obscured the
earlier, more difficult, but finer methods of meading, and so
all of them, including the ciders (with one exception) are
brewed.   Even so these meads were esteemed highly, just as
certain wines prepared with heat have been.   This is seen
in the names attached to his recipes, where it will be observed
that the great ones of the land prided themselves upon their
own recipes for making their metheglins.   Here is a selection
from the titles of his recipes—

White Metheglin of My Lady Hungerford : Which is Exceedingly
    praised.
The Countess of Bullingbrook's White Metheglin.

My Lady Gower's White Meathe used at Salisbury.
Sir Thomas Gower's Metheglin for Health.
My Lord Hollis Hydromel.
My Lady Morices Meath.
My Lady Morice Her Sister makes her's thus :
Sir William Paston's Meathe.
Sir Baynam Throckmorton's Meathe.
My Lady Bellassises Meath.
To Make White Metheglin of Sir John Fortescue.
My Lord Gorge His Meathe.
The Lady Vernon's White Metheglin.
Sir John Arundel's White Meath.
To Make White Metheglin of the Countess of Dorset.
My Lord Herbert's Meath.
The Earl of Denbigh's Metheglin.
Metheglin or Sweet Drink of My Lady Stuart.
A Metheglin for the Colick and Stone of the Same Lady.
A Receipt for Metheglin of My Lady Windebanke.
Another of the Same Lady.

There emerges from the pages of Sir Kenelm Digby's book, the fact that one of the leading devotees of mead was the Queen Mother, to whose cause Sir Kenelm was loyal all his life. Thus we find the recipe entitled—*Hydromel as I made it weak for the Queen Mother*, of which he goes on to say— " Thus was the Hydromel made that I gave the Queen, which was exceedingly liked by everybody."

From the pages of Sir Kenelm Digby comes out the conception (which we have seen in earlier times was associated plainly with mead), one quotation thereon we have made earlier, wherein he attributed the great age, and the large family, of a worthy Chief Burgomaster of Antwerp to his frequent quaffing of goblets of mead. The title of another of his recipes carries the same implications—" An Excellent way to make Metheglin, Called the Liquor of Life." While in writing of " Mr. Pierce's Excellent White Metheglin " he returns to the same subject—

" This Metheglin is a great Balsom and strengthener of the *Viscera* ; is excellent in colds and coughs and consumptions. For which last they used to burn it (like wine) or rather onely heat it. Then dissolve the yolk of an Egge or two in a Pint of it, and some fresh Butter, and drink it warm in the morning fasting. As it comes from the

Barrel or Bottle, it is used to be drunk a large draught (without any alteration or admixtion), with a toste early in the morning (eating the toste) when they intend to dine late."

As regards the last point, they were certainly men in those days, when, instead of our anaemic tea or coffee and toast, with an egg and bacon if the Food Minister will permit it, our ancestors drained off a large draught of mead, nibbling a toast with it, for their breakfast, and thus fortified sallied forth into the world. At any rate what they drank was wholesome, and, in all reason, they had every right to believe in its qualities, even if it was not the complete heal-all that some of them would have made it out to be.

Mead, however, was not only considered good for man, but it was even recommended in the setting of seeds in husbandry, as we learn from a work of the preceding century where we read—" They say they will be verie pleasant, if the seede be steeped in meadth." [157]

Although at this time mead was in its decline, its manufacture was not restricted to this country—to the houses of the great epicures, as well as to the cottage of the humble bee-keeper, where it lived on longest in the end—for Sir Kenelm Digby gives us more than one foreign recipe. We read in the pages of his delightful book of—" Metheglin as it is made at Liége, Communicated by Mr. Masillon ", and of the recipe of " Mr. Corsellises Antwerp Meath ", and, again, of the recipe of " Meath from the Muscovian Ambassadour's Steward ".

We learn in connection with Mr. Corsellise's Antwerp mead that, as in the case of the grape, it was realized that the part of the country from which the raw material of the liquor came had effect on the quality, for we read—" To make good Meath, good white and thick Marsilian or Provence-Honey is best."

Incidentally, it is of interest to note, in connection with the types of mead, that *Mr. Corsellises Antwerp Meath* would appear to have been of a dry quality.

In the pages of Pepys and Sir Kenelm Digby we probably

find the last mentions of the appearance of mead at Court, or in connection with Court personages, although there is no reason why it should not have lasted on till the coming of the Hanoverians, whose appearance would be sufficient to stifle any old English culture still surviving at Court. Dryden, who lived in the latter half of the seventeenth century, was certainly acquainted with it, for he writes—

> " T' allay the strength and harshness of the wine
> Let with old Bacchus, new Metheglin join."

Mead, although becoming a steadily rarer liquor, was still held in regard by the gentry even after these times. For we read (under the year 1712) of its being on sale at the new Spring-Garden at Vauxhall in Addison's *Coverley Papers* : [158]

" We were now arrived at *Spring-Garden*, which is exquisitely pleasant at this time of the year. When I considered the fragrancy of the walks and bowers, with the choirs of birds that sung upon the trees, and the loose tribe of people that walked under their shades, I could not but look upon the place as a kind of *Mahometan* paradise. Sir Roger told me it put him in mind of a little coppice by his house in the country, which his chaplain used to call an aviary of nightingales. *You must understand,* says the Knight, *there is nothing in the world that pleases a man in love so much as your nightingale. Ah, Mr.* Spectator ! *the many moonlight nights that I have walked by myself, and thought on the widow by the musick of the nightingale !* He here fetched a deep sigh, and was falling in to a fit of musing, when a mask, who came behind him, gave him a gentle tap upon the shoulder, and asked him if he would drink a bottle of mead with her ? But the Knight, being startled at so unexpected a familiarity, and displeased to be interrupted in his thoughts of the widow, told her, *She was a wanton baggage,* and bid her go about her business."

In a foreword dedicated to Queen Anne, we find Joseph Warder, a physician and bee-keeper, of 1726, writing in praise of mead, and saying, that it is a liquor in " no ways inferior to the best wines coming either from France or Spain ".

Of much the same times (1747) we still read of mead in various connections, such as in *Mrs. Delany, Life and Correspondence,* [159] where we have—" He begs a thousand acknowledgements to you for all favours, particularly the meath." While we find that in 1771, according to Smollett, [160] the knowledge of making his own mead was still considered one of the arts of country gentlemen.   He tells us of the landowner who had returned to his impoverished and dilapidated estate, and with the aid of a neighbour restored it to prosperity again, and, in the course of doing so, was taught by this neighbour how " to brew beer, to make cyder, perry, mead, usquebaugh, and plague-water ; to cook several outlandish delicacies, such as *ollas*, *pepper-pots*, *pillaws*, *corys*, *chabobs*, and *stufatas* ". But as late as the next generation a poet [161] could still be found to sing of this ancient liquor not yet quite unfamiliar to common knowledge in many parts of England—" The good mead did its good office soon."

We have seen in the process of one thousand years, throughout which we have been able to trace references to mead from the times of Beowulf and the Court of King Arthur to that of Charles II, that while mead starts and ends a royal drink, at the end it is almost exclusively used by the King and the upper classes and is no longer in that general usage whereby everyone might expect on high occasions to partake of it.

Yet, fortunately, the making of real mead has never quite died out.   The late Rev. Tickner Edwardes in his masterly little book *The Bee-Master of Warrilow* describes the wine of an old Sussex bee-master.   The bottle, covered with cobwebs, contained a sparkling wine which was, to him, like sparkling hock with a suggestion of Sherry in it.   While my own meads and sack-meads have all the qualities of fine wines, and I know a choice few who make their meads with all the care bestowed upon a chateau-bottled French wine of the finest vintage.

CHAPTER VIII

CAUSES OF THE DECLINE OF MEAD

THE more one studies the history and use of mead, and the more one samples this liquor, the more we understand why it was considered in all ancient mythology the drink of the gods, and the liquor of the nobles. This fact instantly demands an explanation for the decline of so precious a liquor, a decline which is not merely a question of a fall in popularity, but a fall so low that its very name is but a name to nearly all, except those fortunate few who have still their own meads and metheglins.[162]

No single cause can account for this disappearance of mead from the high table : there must have been many forces at work contributing to this result.

One of these was the change over to sweet wines, which must have led to a degeneration in the character of mead. This significant change in English wine taste took place in the fifteenth century when we turned away from the dry wines of France, such as Claret and Burgundy, to the sweet wines. This change was maintained right through the sixteenth century and by the seventeenth century little French wine entered the country. Whilst in the eighteenth and nineteenth centuries we all know the high estimation (unjustified as it might have been) of Port, Sherry, Madeira and other sweet wines.

This fashion for a sweet wine was bound to influence the simple bee-master making his small barrel of mead. Furthermore, it is a significant fact that the more untrained the palate the more it prefers a sweet wine. Therefore the survival of mead-making mainly among the peasantry, whose palates would tend to favour a sweet liquor, meant that with these changes in the wine-taste of this country the drink as made was bound to become unduly sweet and coarse with the passage of time.

Invariably as a taste for very sweet wines develops, there is a demand for stronger flavours to give interest to the syrupy liquor. Consequently, as sweet, sack-mead, among the few who made it, became more popular than mead, and as sack-mead itself was drunk newer and sweeter, so a tendency towards the spicing of it was bound to develop. Thus the taste for a sack-mead where it is uncultivated leads inevitably to the making of a sweet, sack-metheglin, and so the appreciation of the more subtle bouquet of mead, and well-matured sack-mead, becomes vitiated.

This has meant that whenever, during the centuries in which this degeneration has occurred, discriminating drinkers by chance came to taste what they thought was mead, it was much less to their liking than real mead would have been. This led to that complete neglect which allowed its making not only to pass into the hands of the peasantry entirely, but to remain uninfluenced by the demands of people of taste, and that meant in turn that the liquor degenerated more and more, until the present product made of herbs, hops, spices, honey and even raisins, arose—a shabby pretender never drunk by the gods in Valhalla or by the nobles in Tara's halls.

But, as we have already seen, there was another, and overriding, factor which was bound to cause the gradual decline in the quantity of mead which could be drunk, and that was the shrinkage in the supplies of honey. As the quantity of honey declined, the less mead was made, the more expensive it became, and the more it was restricted to the tables of the great, until, at the end, it was the drink only of the Courts and the richer people on the one hand, and, at the other end of the social scale, of the peasants who were too poor to buy wine, but who were always able to make their own small keg of mead or metheglin, from the washings of the combs, after the bulk of the honey had been squeezed out and sold. That was the position, in no small measure, by Tudor times, and it only required the misadventure of suffering from the influence of

the ill-tastes in wine of the age and of the monarch, to destroy
the art of what mead-making was still left in the country.

The further, and ultimate, blow at mead- and metheglin-
making in the last fifty years or so, where it had still lingered
on among some of the peasantry, was not only due to that
collapse of good housekeeping which both Cobbett and Druit
(to whom we shall refer presently) deplore, but to the invention of the modern beehive. The modern hive is fitted with
movable combs, which, when the honey crop is taken, are
removed, and put into a machine by the aid of which the
honey is thrown out of the cells, and then the same combs
are put back in the hive for the bees to refill ; and so the
same wax and the same comb, getting heavier in wax, and
more and more discoloured from use, is used year after year
by the bees and their master. But, in the old days, bees
were kept in straw skeps, and the combs in these skeps are as
they are naturally built by the bees, and they cannot be
replaced by man once they have been removed. Therefore
when the bee-master had removed the bees, he cut the combs
out of the skep, and squeezed out as much honey as he could,
as is still done with heather honey which is too thick to
extract by machinery, and when he had done this he was left
with a mass of sticky, honey-saturated beeswax. To avoid
wasting this unsaleable honey, and in order to clean the wax,
he put the mass into a vessel of pure well-water, and continued to add more wax and honey until he had a liquor of
sufficient strength, and from this his mead or metheglin was
made. But, with the invention of the new hive, once he
could sell all his honey he did so, partly because of the decline
in good housekeeping generally, and partly because the
peasant was so poor that he preferred a few extra shillings
to a keg of liquor.

Needless to say, had there been an adequate supply of
honey in Tudor times, the art of mead-making would have
been in many hands, in those not only of Court and peasant,
but also in those of nobles, squires, monasteries, yeomen and
vintners, and, whatever the ill-taste of the Tudor age towards

wines generally, the history of mead would have been the same as that of wine, and it would have recovered in the course of time from that imposition of spicings and sweetness which the Tudor period tended to impose upon all our wines.

Therefore in this shrinkage in honey production have we the one fundamental cause of the decline of mead, to which the others were merely contributory.

In Chapter II we have touched upon the gradual shrinkage of honey production in relation to the number of men on the earth, which has been a natural outcome of the increase of population and civilization. We saw that at the beginning of historic times there were wide woods and pastures throughout northern Europe, and the lindens, chestnuts, acacias, thorns and field flowers hummed with bees in their seasons, and the natural wild bee population was at its greatest, while the men were few. But as time passed the human increased, and, as a result, the amount of wild honey declined compared with the numbers of men. This was offset, to some extent, so far as the stocks available to early man were concerned, by the domestication of the bee, but this did not increase the actual amount of nectar being sucked by the bees from the flowers—that could not be increased by domestication. In point of fact, the total amount of nectar being collected must have been declining, even at that very time when man was, temporarily, increasing his own supplies by the domestication of the bee. For, at the same time, he was putting the axe to the great trees which provided nectar, and was putting the plough into the fields, and planting in the place of wild flowers, grain plants which yield no nectar for the honey bee. Thus, as settlement and civilization spread, so inexorably the yield of honey tended to decline, and once man had profited by his first gains by the domestication of the bee, his supplies also steadily fell.

All the data we have available tells of this ever-increasing cost of honey (and so of mead) and its greater rise in cost as time passed compared with that of wine.

For example, honey in the eleventh century was 6d. to 7d. a

gallon (12d. to 13d. a sextary : i.e. a large sextary—*cum majori mensura*—not a small sextary of 15 pints), and in the thirteenth century it sold at 7d. a gallon, and in the fourteenth century at 1s. 2d.

This would mean that the honey content of each gallon of mead would cost, in the eleventh century 2$\frac{1}{4}d$., in the thirteenth century 2$\frac{1}{2}d$., and in the fourteenth century 5$\frac{1}{4}d$. All the other costs in manufacturing the mead would send the price up two or three or four times these figures. Thorold Rogers (from whom the above figures have been quoted) also gives the price of mead selling at Cambridge in 1682 as " 2 bottle @ 1s." and as selling in 1702 at 2s. 4d. a gallon. These prices are consistent with this general trend.[163]

In comparison with these mead costs we find that in the thirteenth century Gascon, Auxerre, France and Moselle wines were coming in at a rate of between $\frac{3}{4}d$. and 3$\frac{1}{2}d$. a gallon. By the fourteenth century Gascon wine (which was 90 per cent of our imports) was priced at 3$\frac{1}{2}d$. a gallon, although at London in 1338 it went as high as 4$\frac{1}{4}d$. Rhine wine at the same time cost from 6d. to 1s. 2d.[164]

From this it is clear that the dearest Gascon wine was selling a penny cheaper a gallon than the raw materials of a like quantity of mead ! A mead could hardly have been sold for less than 11d. a gallon, and was probably nearer 1s. 6d. a gallon, as against the Gascon wine at 3$\frac{1}{2}d$. to 4$\frac{1}{4}d$. !

We have a check on the price of mead by a comparison of its values with ale. We find that there was a recognized scale of values whereby four casks of ale were reckoned equivalent to two casks of spiced ale, or one cask of mead.[165]

Now in the fourteenth century ale was worth 4d. a gallon. In that case mead was worth about 1s. 4d. a gallon—which compares with and confirms the computations we have made above, based on the price of honey at this time.

Prices standing thus, whereby mead cost three and a half times as much as the normal wine drink, it can be realized that it had ceased to be the daily drink of all except the wealthy or those who kept their own bee-gardens, as did the monasteries and the great houses. The only wines which appear to have been more expensive were the rare (and therefore costly) Cretan (4s. in 1360) and Italian Vernage (2s. in 1335 at Durham).

Mead was therefore much more expensive than ordinary wine and classed with the costlier. That is why the Priest Absolon gives the lady in the *Miller's Tale* mead, and that is why it is mentioned by Chaucer as a sacrificial wine in one connection, and in another, with costly spices.

Not only would this ever-increasing rise in the cost be a principal cause of removing mead from general use, but it also had a secondary effect. It influenced the type of mead. Mead has a great advantage over wine as the mead-maker can decide the strength and sweetness of his liquor before he starts manufacturing it. This means that as mead could not compete in price with cheap French wines the mead-maker had to concentrate upon sack-mead, since the only rivals to sack-mead were the expensive sweet Italian (Vernage), Cretan, Malmsey, and other southern European wines.

Thus it came about that as the quantity of mead available shrank, it tended to become more and more a sack-mead. The same effect must have been felt in the manufacture of spiced mead or metheglin.

Another and very important factor which was bound to affect adversely a bee-keeping industry, the position of which was becoming progressively more difficult, was the interruption to security and normal life brought about by great political upheavals, such as, for example, the Reformation and, in Germany, the Thirty Years' War. We have already seen, in the case of Eger, in Bohemia, the significant drop from thirteen mead-houses before the Reformation and the Thirty Years' War to one afterwards.

Indeed, we may marvel that the mead industry continued so late, and so vigorously, as the Middle Ages, and we can only account for this by the special needs of the Church before the Reformation. The demand of the mediaeval Church for wax candles was undoubtedly an important factor in arresting the gradual and inevitable decline of honey production, especially as from the later Middle Ages onwards honey was no longer the only source of sweetness, for sugar, with other spices, was then beginning to arrive from overseas. Hilda M. Ransome [166] points out that in one church alone in the Middle Ages on a great feast day sixty candles were burnt on the high altar, while in the chief church of Wittenburg there was used 35,000 lb. of wax a year! Every church and monastery had bee-houses, and at one such, Kloster Neustadt, there were 300 stocks. It was usual, because of this demand for wax, for feudal dues and tithes to be demanded in wax. The Reformation, which took place mainly in that part of Europe outside of the wine-making regions, where the bee and not the vine was the source of liquor, saw an end of all that. Thus the Reformation, unwittingly, was a prime cause in banishing mead from our tables! For no longer was it so worthwhile to hunt the forests, and pull out the wax and honey from every crack and crevice in the trees and rocks where wild stocks of honey bees had laid it, and no longer were stocks taken into the forest to hoard all the precious nectar from the trees, or up into the hills, on to moors, downs and heaths for the same purpose. Half the profit in bee-keeping went, when the lights ceased to blaze on the high altar, and before the figures of the saints. As if this were not enough, but at this very period, honey was faced for the first time in European history, with a rival, a cheap substitute, in the form of sugar, which had begun to arrive in ever-increasing quantities from the fifteenth century onwards, and the arrival of which was now reaching serious proportions.

The bottom fell clean out of the market, and so the natural trend which was towards a decline in honey production (and so of mead) for every head of population in any case, through the shrinkage of the natural bee-forage and the inordinate increase of mankind, unrestrainedly reasserted itself, and ultimately honey was produced only as a luxury by the cottager, for selling to the rich. The cottager found it more profitable to sell it than to turn it into mead, what little he made was for himself from the washings of the combs, and when the honey reached the buyer it was too costly to turn into liquor when wine could be bought for less. By the time the peasant had ceased to use the straw skep, even he, as we have already seen, stopped making his mead and metheglin.

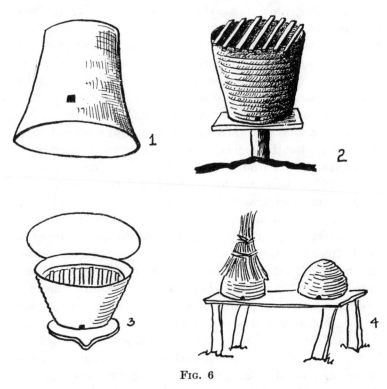

FIG. 6

Ancient Types of Beehives

1. Cypriot ; 2 and 3. Ancient Greek ; 4. The common skephive in use in England before the invention of the wooden frame hive. One is covered with a straw hackle to give extra protection to the bees

That the Reformation had this disastrous effect upon mead production would seem to be supported by the continued popularity of mead of one form or another in Poland down to the present day. In Cracow, for instance, in 1939 there were many old taverns, such as the " Under the Little Cross

Tavern " (*Pod Krzyzykiem*), a fashionable haunt of the university and the town, where *miód*, mead, was the sole or chief liquor served. As Poland is the only large country of Western Europe outside the wine-producing lands which remained unreformed the survival of a mead-making industry is significant. The survival of mead in Russia and other eastern countries not subject to the influence of the Reformation would appear to support this conclusion. Ukrainian soldiers, in the First World War, were frequent patrons of it, and much mead, is, or was, made in western Russia down to the present time. It is a common feature to read in travellers' accounts of Russia of the making and drinking of mead.[167]

Curiously enough, the history of honey production has reached another turning point in its history—for two new factors have altered the whole position. The first is the discovery of new countries overseas, which provide more bee-forage than their own populations can readily consume, or will be likely to consume for a century, and from this source alone all the honey that is needed for some time can be met, even if, as is likely, the consumption of honey should continue to increase. Thus, as in the time of Richard II (1380) when we imported honey from the Continent, we have been importing honey from New Zealand, Australia, California and elsewhere to meet the needs of this country. This import of overseas honey, under normal conditions of trade, depressed the prices of British honey without making it unremunerative to produce, since our honey was still able to command a higher price than the imported honey. All this has tended to keep the raw material of mead down to an economical price.

The second new factor in the provision of an adequate supply of honey lies in the improved methods of growing bee-forage. It is now possible to grow crops, such as various clovers, which, while providing the fodder for which they are primarily intended, can increase the nectar supplies considerably.

Therefore, from these two sources, a greater supply of

honey is assured than for many centuries, and this will stave off for a long time, as the Church's demand for wax did throughout the Middle Ages, the shrinkage of our honey resources.

Wine and mead are quite different in their response to this increase of mankind on the earth. As man spreads he is able to increase his vineyards, and so wine has never had to face these troubles which have beset mead. But curiously enough man himself has interposed, so far as this country is concerned, a factor favourable to mead and disadvantageous to its rival. Governments, in their search for revenue, have placed heavier and heavier import duties upon wines, which have forced the prices upwards. Then again wine has to be bought from the vineyards, gathered into stores, shipped, and then distributed from the ports throughout the country. All these costs which do not fall upon a home-made liquor have increased considerably as a result of recurrent wars and rising costs of living. Therefore, no matter how unkindly history has been towards mead, the situation has changed radically, and the best mead can be made now for no more than wine, and indeed for less.

CHAPTER IX

SACK, SACK-MEAD AND SHERRIS SACK

AT this point it is necessary to clear up some confusion in the use of the term sack, which is one used for certain types of mead as well as for particular wines.

We have seen that there are reasons for believing that in early times the mead was drunk strong and sweet, because, before the knowledge of storing and ageing liquor was achieved, the mead was drunk new, and such a liquor was known to the primitive Aryans as *mead* (*madhu*). Such a new mead would be of full alcoholic strength, and, although it would be sweet, had it been kept in cask and bottle sufficiently long, it would have become quite dry. We must not, therefore, imagine that the primitive mead was necessarily a mead of excessive sweetness, although it is reasonably certain that in many instances it would be.

Because of the ever-increasing cost of honey there would in early times be a tendency to weaken the mead which was used for everyday use, and it has been suggested that this was the origin of ale, the name of which is probably an old word for mead.

There is also a possibility that among our own ancestors there was an attempt to distinguish not merely the weak meads, as *ales*, but also the strong sweet meads as *biuzas* or *beers*.

With the introduction into the Aryan world of the knowledge of malting, malt was first added to the honey in the making of ale, and eventually was used entirely, so that early Anglo-Saxon ale, while having some of the quality of a light mead, had, nevertheless, ceased to be a mead.

When the knowledge of beer (which is not merely made from malt, but was exceedingly strong and made with herbs) reached the north from Egypt, its strength in alcohol and its strong taste made it a cheap substitute for the most expensive and strongest mead, which we have assumed was called *biuza* or *beer*, and it, thereupon, as *ale* had also done, assumed the name which rightly belonged to mead, but in this case to a strong mead.

It thus came about that the word mead was left to perform a generalized function (which it no doubt always had done) of denoting all types of mead, and it lost any chance of developing a specialized meaning for that intermediate type of mead which was still sweet when fermenting, but which when old was dry, and which was neither called *ale* nor *biuza* nor *beer*.

Thus it comes about that we can never be certain of the strength and qualities of the meads which come down to us in old accounts except where the context gives us some assistance.

A typical example of this general and unprecise use of the word *mead* is to be found in Samuel Purchas, a seventeenth-century writer, who, speaking of mead production in Russia talks of " meade of all sorts ".

We have seen also a further source of confusion in the introduction of the word *metheglin* as an alternative for mead, although it ought to be used solely for a spiced mead.

To overcome this confusion there grew up (perhaps as early as the late Middle Ages) the entirely laudable practice of speaking of *sack-mead* when reference to a dessert mead was made as distinct from the " sparkling mead " of Taliesin, or the crystal goblet of old mead offered to Loki, both of which, by their context, suggest the light meads akin to the beverage wines of to-day. How old this practice is, is difficult to say, but it is well over a hundred years old [168] and as I have suggested it may indeed go right back to the late Middle Ages and Tudor times, when the use of sack was very common. Sir Kenelm Digby, the seventeenth-century writer upon mead, comes very close to associating mead and sack in one of his recipes (that of *Sack with Clove-Gilly Flowers*), where he goes on to amplify his recipe by saying, " Upon better consideration : I conceive the best way of making Hydromel with Clove-gilly flowers is thus " from which it seems evident that he equated in his mind this particular mead (hydromel) with Sack.[169]

The word sack is said to be derived from *seco*, meaning dry [170] as Sherry is said to be the English variant of *Xeres*. It was used not only for Spanish wines. The wines of Canary, Malaga, Xeres were all called sacks.

But if the use of the term sack for a sweet mead is the traditional usage, it would throw some doubt upon whether this usually accepted derivation of sack is correct and would lend support to the much more reasonable explanation offered by T. G. Shaw, who says :

> " There is no doubt that considerable quantities of these [i.e. Canary and similar wines] wines, under the name of Canary Sack, were brought to this country even three hundred years ago. And, as there is sometimes allusion to ' sack with sugar ', and even to ' sacke sweete ', and the same is applied to ' Malaga sack ' and ' Sherris sack ', it is evident that the word ' sack ' cannot be understood to have denoted *sec* (dry)." [171]

And again he remarks :

> " The more we investigate, the more do we find preconceived ideas and theories overturned by unwelcomed facts, which nullify opinions that appeared well-founded and have been received as axioms. It has long appeared to me very doubtful whether the wine we now call sherry, from Xerez, was known in this country, even 150 years ago. I can trace no authority for it, except the words in Shakespeare, ' sherris sack ', which is usually supposed to be ' dry sherry ' ; but we find also in old books, ' sack with sugar ', and sack in so many ways, that it is evidently not derived from the French word ' *sec*', dry." [172]

The Malaga of repute to this day is a sweet wine, and it seems hard to escape the conclusion that Malaga sack, a favourite beverage, must refer to the better, and sweet, Malaga.

We will remember, in this connection, that Falstaff quaffed cups of Canary sack and Madeira as well as Sherris sack (at the cost of 2s. 8d. a gallon !) which he sweetened with sugar bought for the purpose. Now it is much easier to produce a sweet wine than a dry one, as anyone knows who has tried, and it would seem passing strange to buy a wine made purposely dry and then sweeten it, when a sweet wine could be commanded easily enough, which did not require such treatment.   But a sweet wine, in an age with a sweet tooth, such as the Elizabethan, might well be made sweeter.

That the Spanish wines were strong wines, and therefore very likely to have been sweet, would appear from what Chaucer says in the *Pardoner's Tale*, which contains a diatribe against the strong heady Sherry :

> " Now kepe yow fro the white and fro the rede,
> And namely fro the whité wyn of Lepe, [Lepe near Cadiz.]
> That is to selle in Fysshstrete, or in Chepe.   [Fleet-street.]
> This wyn of Spaigné crepeth subtilly
> In othere wynés growynge fasté by,
> Of which ther ryseth swich fumositee,
> That when a man hath dronken draughtés thre,
> And weneth that he be at hoom in Chepe,
> He is in Spaigné right at the toune of Lepe,—
> Nat at the Rochele, ne at Burdeux-toun." [173]

The statement of Sir Kenelm Digby, writing in the seventeenth century, in his recipe—*My own Considerations for Making of Meathe*, where he says " some good *sweet* White-wine (as Canary sack) " would seem to be definite enough. He evidently considered *sack* a sweet wine.

From all this it does not look as though the Spanish and related wines were *seco*.

Knowing the taste for sweetness in earlier times, it does not seem that the learned Dionysius Petavius (1659) could possibly have described the exports of the Canary Islands as " *sublime* sacks, fine sugars, and canary-birds " if these wines had been dry.[174]

In support of the statement that our forebears particularly admired sweet wines it will be shown, later, that despite a connection between the *ancient* Clarets and the *clarre* wine of Chaucer, this latter wine was made sweet deliberately (although claret to-day is a dry wine) by the addition of honey.

Furthermore, women, with few exceptions, prefer sweet to dry wines, and one must suppose that this preference was the more marked when wines in general tended to be sweeter than they are now. That being so it is significant when we find in old, and we fear, often abandoned, tavern songs of the

FIG. 7

Seventeenth-century Sack Bottle

Tudor period, the man's mistress is referred to as, or likened to, *sack*.

> " There have I Mistress got,
> Cloyster'd in a Pottle-pot ;
> Plump and bouncing, soft, and fair,
> Buxsome sweet, and debonnair,
> And they call her, Sack my dear." [175]

The use of Sack in such a connection, whether it refers to the hussy's tipple, or to her quality of agreeableness, makes inescapable the conclusion that a sweet, sugary, honeyed condition is envisaged.

In view of these facts it would seem reasonable to suggest that sack is a corruption of the Latin *saccharum*, meaning sweet, and that all the sweet wines were classified as sacks. It has, therefore, nothing whatever to do with *sec*, *seco*, or dry.

In that event the sweet meads were equally sacks, and indeed where sack only is mentioned without any qualification we do not know for certain that sweet mead is not being referred to as much as any other sweet wine.

Thus, in fact, it could well be to a sack-mead that reference is made when we read in *The Merry Wives of Windsor* [176] of " sack and wine and metheglin ", although in this instance it was more likely a wine sack to which reference is made. It certainly is in Sir J. Mennis' *Musarum* (1655), where we read—"While there's a cider-man or a metheglinist, . . . I do forswear of wicked sack."

It is quite possible that it was the shrinkage in the amount of sweet mead which could be made, owing to the gradual decline in its production, that led to the increasing import of sweet wines from the thirteenth and fourteenth centuries onwards.

Therefore, in using the already established term sack-mead for a sweet mead no appropriation of a wine name is being perpetrated, since the term sack is merely used to denote a sweet liquor, although, it is readily admitted, that it is more frequently associated with Spanish, Canary, and like types of wines.

CHAPTER X

MULSUM, PYMENT, CLARRE, HIPPOCRAS, BRACKET AND OTHER ANCIENT DRINKS RELATED TO MEAD

IN Roman times a dessert and aperitif wine was made by mixing wine· and honey and water and this was called *mulsum*.[177] In other words this was a form of mead and wine mixed. Columella [178] tells us the proportions were four parts of wine to one of honey. Virgil [179] has an obvious reference to mulsum when he says that bees make the clear, sweet honey which is used to make mild harsh-flavoured wine. It was drunk at the beginning of the meal, much as we now use an aperitif, and then at the end as a dessert wine. The Greeks had the same wine which they called *melitités* (μελῑτίτης).

Another honey wine of the Romans was *myritis*, made from honey, old wine, and myrtle berries. *Melomeli*, too, was a wine made from honey and fruit juices, and, in principle, is not far removed from the early ciser made in England in the Middle Ages.

The Romans also made several medicinal drinks from honey, and although they do not rightly belong to a discussion upon mead and wine they ought to be mentioned in passing. Of these medicinal liquors was one compounded of unfermented honey water, which they called *aqua mulsa*. Another was *oxymel*, of honey, vinegar, salt, and water, and used for throat and ear troubles. It was also employed as a salad dressing. Oxymel appears to have been in common use down to the Middle Ages.[180] For nuptial occasions they had a bouquet liquor composed of honey and milk mixed with poppy juice—a drink calculated to create the utmost of cheerfulness and carefree abandon. The Romans had also another liquor called *clionomeli* made of whites of eggs and honey, and I assume it was medicinal.   Curiously enough the Romans had genuine mead, *hydromel*, which they would appear often to have as a medicine,[181] much as, in the nineteenth century, we used Port.

Among the Greeks, besides mead, or hydromel, we read of similar strange liquors, derived from honey.   Thus there was *rhodomel*, a mixture of roses and honey, *omphacomel*, which was a kind of grape juice and honey, and a similar liquor compounded of unfermented grape juice called *oenomel*, which was used for gout and nervous ailments.   Besides these there was *kykeon*, a drink made from oil, wine, cheese, and meal, which was drunk at the time of the harvest feast (the feast of boughs).[182]   They also had *thalassiomel* prepared with sea-water!   (The ancients were very peculiar about their water, for we find that Pliny (Bk. XIV, ch. 20) advised the use of five-year-old rain-water.)

In the Middle Ages there was a genuine need in the northern wine-drinking countries for something approaching a dessert wine, and so a drink was made resembling mulsum very closely and this was called variously (in Chaucer for example) *clarre* or *clarree*, and *pyment* or *pigment*.   It consisted of wine and honey (as in the case of mulsum but unlike the Roman drink without the addition of water) and sometimes it would seem that it was also spiced.   As sugar began to come into Europe it came to be compounded more and more of sugar, and this variant (especially when spiced) is what is known as *hippocras*.   Pyment seems to have been the favourite in fourteenth-century England and hippocras in France at that time.   Hippocras came to have the addition of spirits and in that form we have the survival of a form of it in the various proprietary drinks such as Dubonnet and Byrrh.

In England there was always the sack-mead as a dessert wine, but in France (except in the south), where the main reliance was upon the grape, there was a decided lack of a sweeter wine.   As a result there was a complete dependence upon very expensive imported wines from the Mediterranean or else upon hippocras to meet this need. Judging by old French menus of the fourteenth century hippocras was essential as the " Issue " wine—the " Issue " being the last course at which hippocras and wafers and spices were served. Thus we read in a French account of the fourteenth century of the dinner given by Abbot de Lagny in Paris to Monseigneur de Paris, the President, the Procureur, and the Advocat du Roy—" Hippocras and wafers are the issue—Hippocras two quarts (and this is too much, as is aforesaid concerning the [wine of] Grenache), two hundred wafers and sufflications." [183]

Rabelais writes in the following terms of a white hippocras, and in doing so virtually provides a recipe of how hippocras was made :

" Stay till I give you somewhat to drink out of this Nestorian goblet. Will you have another draught of white hippocras ? Be not afraid of the squinzy, no. There is neither squinanthus, ginger, nor grains in it ; only a little choice cinnamon, and some of the best refined sugar, with the delicious white wine of the growth of that vine, which was set in the slips of the great sorb-apple, above the walnut tree." [184]

From Chaucer we gather that hippocras was considered to have a tonic and aphrodisiac quality :

The Wordes of the Hoost to the Phisicien and the Pardoner
" Thyn Ypocras, and eek thy Galiones,
And every boyste ful of thy letuarie : " (Line 306)

. . . .

The Merchant's Tale
" Soone after that, this hastif Januarie
Wolde go to bedde, he wolde no lenger tarye.
He drynketh ypocras, clarree and vernage,
Of spices hoote, tencreesen his crage ;
And many a letuarie hath he ful fyn
Swiche as the cursed monk, Daun Constantyn,
Hath writen in his book, *De Coitu* ; " (Line 1800 ff.)

The powerful stimulating qualities of hippocras probably accounts for the fact that in France it was only drunk in the winter time.

But in England at this time, pyment or clarree rather than

hippocras, as we should expect (in a mead-making country), was drunk.   For this wine, unlike hippocras, was made from honey, and not sugar, as we find in Chaucer, in *Boece*, where he refers to the pyment mixture of wine and honey in the following lines :

> " Blisful was the firste age of men
> They heelden hem apayed with the
> metes that the trewe feeldes broughten
> forth.   They ne destroyeden ne desseyvede
> not hemself with outrage.   They
> weren wont lyghtly to slaken hir hungir
> at even with accornes of ookes.
> *They ne coude not medle the yift of*
> *Bachus to the cleer hony (that is to seyn*
> *they coude make no pyment or clarree),*
> ne they could not medle the bryghte
> fleeses of the contre of Seryens with the
> venym of Tyrie (this is to seyn, thei
> coude nat deyen white fleeses of Syrien
> contre with the blood of a maner schelle-
> fyssche that men fynden in Tyrie, with
> which blood men deyen purpre)."   (Lines Bo. 469–485)

In the *Romaunt of the Rose* Chaucer again refers to the liquor :

> " But ye shull not forsworen be,
> Ne lette, therefore, to drynke clarre
> Or Pyment makid fresh and newe."   (Line R. 6027)

We have already read of another reference by Chaucer to pyment, witnessing to its popularity, where the priest Absolon takes his mead and spiced ale, along with the pyment and piping hot wafers to woo a townswoman.

Pyment appears to have been spelt pigment as well as sometimes being called clarree.[185]   Nevertheless, pyment and clarree are so often spoken of as distinct wines that there must have been some difference between them.   Thus :

> " Mete and drynk they hadde afyn
> Pyement, claré, and Reynysch wyn."

There would seem to be some reason for believing that clarree was originally a Gascon wine mixed with honey, which was shipped from Clairette,[186] the natural wine of which place when shipped without the admixture of honey, being quite dry. As the growths of Clairette were in favour in England the wine of the whole region (Bordeaux) became known as Claret. From the above quotation of Chaucer's *Romaunt of the Rose* it would seem that the English in his time mixed their clarree freshly before drinking, and this would infer that the French, by now, no longer exported their clairette honeyed but only in a dry condition.

The word clarree, therefore, would really be Claret, but meaning in the Middle Ages a pyment and not a dry wine.

As far as we can see clarree is the anglicized French, while pyment is the real English word for this liqueur or cordial wine compounded of honey and Claret. Perhaps it was pyment when made in England, and sold as clarree wine when shipped from France in an already manufactured condition.

Some support for believing that Claret was formerly more robust than it is now, by the addition of honey or sugar, is suggested by the fact that in Scotland Claret was sold by the stoup—a treatment young Port or Sherry could stand but not modern Claret.

The desire for such highly spiced and flavoured wines as pyment and hippocras seems to have increased as time passed, until in Elizabethan times the various kinds of sack began to replace these drinks.

Later still the place of sack was filled by the sweet Ports and equally sweet brown Sherries.

It is because of their high spirit content that Ports and Sherries are such potent, and, to the old particularly, dangerous wines, boding ill for sufferers liable to gout, neuritis and other complaints. Pyment, in contrast, because of its wholesome composition, is the opposite, and it is no wonder to find Warner actually describes his recipe for clarry (clarree or pyment) as " an excellent approved medicine both for the stomach and head of an elderly person ".[187]

Maurice Healy is quite mistaken when he writes : " There

was also a frightful confection called ' Clarre ', which was a compound of red wine and honey and ginger and canel, and must have been about as clear as mud." [188]

Pyment which I have had has always been beautifully clear and the colour improved by the slight tawniness given to it from the honey. As regards its being a " frightful confection " that is a question of taste, and whilever modern man drinks Ports, Sherries, Vermouths, and Dubonnets it is clear there is a place for sweet and spiced wines as there was in the past. Furthermore, there is a place, and a time in the day, when these various sweeter drinks are not merely permissible but even desirable.

That our ancestors did not drink these liquors when " as clear as mud " is evident from a fifteenth-century recipe for pyment which runs as follows : " Take clowis, quibibus, maces, canel, galyngale, and make a powdyr thereof, temprying it with good wine and the third part of hony, *and clense hem thorow a clene klothe*." [189]

Sir Kenelm Digby describes a species of pyment, under one title of " Meath with Raisins", in his book so full of mead recipes of Stuart times.

" Saragossa " wine, described by Edward Spencer, is evidently another variant of this ancient pyment, as it is described as being made from wine, to which has been added (for every quart of wine) a sprig of rue, a handful of fennel roots and three pounds of honey.[190]

Prominent, and indeed famous, among those liquors closely related to mead is what, for want of a more specific name, one would call raspberry sack-mead. This, as a sweet liquor, was greatly prized in Poland before the late war. One old writer quoted by Edward Spencer [191] tells of its being obtainable in Sweden, Muscovy, and as far as the Caspian Sea. This consists of the juice of raspberries and honey fermented together. It is by no means an easy liquor to make, as there is a strong tendency to vinegrate unless it is made with skill and care.

Another drink of early times similar to the Roman mulsum

was morat, which was a mixture not of wine, but mulberry juice and honey. This is a drink involving very much the same principles as those involved in making Alicante wine, for Dionisius Petavius tells us of Alicante—" whence is true Alicant Wine made of the juice of Mulberries, plentifully growing here ".[192]

Birch wine of which we read in the seventeenth century involved the same principle of mixing honey with a juice or wine, although the wine is of no great antiquity. In this case the honey was mixed with the juice obtained by tapping the rising sap in the birch tree and boiling them together.[193]

Pytheas tells us [194] that in Thule there was brewed a drink from grain and honey. This would appear to be an early version of bracket [195] which was made on the same lines as mulsum. Instead of wine, the best of ale was used and mixed with honey. To those who have never tasted bracket there is a pleasure in store—as it is one of the smoothest drinks possible. We read about it in the Mabinogion :

> " Though thou get this, there is yet
> That which thou wilt not get.
> Honey that is nine times sweeter
> Than the honey of the virgin
> Swarm, without scum and bees, do
> I require to make bragget for the feast." [196]

While in Chaucer, in *The Miller's Tale*, we read of the carpenter's wife who " sikerly she hadde a likerous eye " and who was courted by the two wicked clerks Nicolas and Absolon the parish priest, that :

" Hire mouth was sweete as bragot or the meeth,
  Or hoard of apples leyd in hey or heeth." (Lines 3261-2)

Curiously enough this mixture of mead and ale to make bracket, bragget, or bragot was frowned upon by the Church, and at three Councils (Aachen in 817, Worms in 868, and Tribur in 895) the custom was strongly condemned.[197] The reason for this is not clear, but it might have been because the mixture was being put on the market as mead.

Many Lancashire towns were famous for their bracket,

among these being Bury, Leigh, and Altcar, and it was especially drunk on mid-Lent Sunday, which was called, as a
consequence, " Braggot Sunday ".

Another little known drink is *bochet* [198] which involves
boiling honey and then diluting it, and it is a sort of " burnt "
sack-mead, but it is probably French and not English, for
it seems to have been made the speciality, in particular, of
the order of Cluny, for whom it was *potus dulcissimus*, and
who used it during great Church festivals. It was given to
the sick and weakly especially, as we used to give a good
Port wine, and so it is a tribute to the value of a mead drink
that the French, despite all their good wines, should have
still turned to a honey-wine for this purpose.

Another variety of mead, or rather we should say metheglin,
is the Polish *miodomel*, a mead flavoured with hops, which
was a speciality of the Polish Monks of St. Basil.

Krupnik was another Polish drink, but hardly a mead,
as it was a whisky boiled with honey, which was drunk hot
during the cold weather.

There is another drink, this time Russian, of which we
know little, but which would seem to be rather a form of
mead, as it is made from linden honey, and is known as
Lipez. [199]

Finally, among the drinks which belong to the mead group
because they are traditionally compounded of mead or honey,
wholly or in part, are certain liqueurs.   These are preparations
of honey, water, and herbs, and among these liqueurs we may
mention maraschino (from the kernels of the Marasca cherry,
a few peach stones, and honey), ratafia of Turin and the
Arsenzia of Switzerland. Chartreuse, when it was making
its reputation, was also made with honey.

From honey it is possible, as might be supposed, to make
an *aquavitae* by distillation. In flavour it is quite unlike any
of the existing types of spirits, coming closest perhaps, *in
flavour*, to some of the Italian brandies, but without their
harshness. Indeed, it is wonderously soft, with the qualities
of the best wine brandies.

Metheglin brandy (as distinct from mead brandy) used to be made by old bee-masters in France, if it is still not being made, and mead brandy still survives in some other countries, while, recently, a revival of the industry is being set on foot in this country.

The knowledge of distilling is very old, and it is possible that besides malting the grain for making beer, actual distillation is inferred by Pliny's remarks already quoted in Chapter II. In the great song of mead by the Welsh bard Taliesin we read of " sparkling distilled mead ". This may only be poetic fancy elaborating the great qualities of mead. On the other hand it is always possible that *distilled* mead was made, and that the poet had this in mind, as well as mead (in the " foaming meadhorns ") when he wrote his poem, in the sixth century. Fairley [200] at any rate takes it in this sense, and quotes it as the first instance of distillation in Britain. He also draws attention to the distillation of a liquor from fermented grain in Ireland in ancient times. This art, according to Irish legend, is supposed to have been taught them by St. Patrick, but whether this indicates it was of a late origin in Ireland or not it is hard to say—as so much is attributed to that saint.

We ought not to forget that very much earlier, in the Vedas of the ancient Aryans, we read of the magical *amrita*, the essence of the *soma*. It is possible that this is some form of a distilled mead. Certainly the origin of distillation is lost in the mists of the past. The ancient Chinese are believed to have had a knowledge of it, and *arrack* was made in India in 800 B.C. Therefore, whether those who would see in the statements of Pliny and Taliesin evidence of distillation are right or not, it makes little difference to the great likelihood that this art was known at the dawn of history in these islands, and, if so, a distillate of honey is not at all unlikely. But whatever and wherever its origin mead brandy is an excellent spirit, and, rare as it may be, it ought not to be left out of any list of mead liquors.

From this review of all the liquors made wholly or partly

from honey it will be seen that, like the grape, honey furnishes all the drinking requirements of man, from the dry sackmeads and old-fashioned cisers, as aperitifs, to dry meads and strong full-bodied dessert sacks, sparkling meads for use like Champagne, and mead liqueurs and brandies as the fitting finish to any repast.   While with the vine, the bee shares in the parentage of those many useful and rare drinks which were once in so much favour, such as pyment and mulsum. John Barleycorn is too coarse and boisterous to compete service by service, and on all occasions, with the juice of the grape or the nectar of the flowers, and they alone are for those evening hours when mind and fancy combined with taste bring to man snatches of the golden age.

CHAPTER XI

PEASANT MEAD AND METHEGLIN

W E ought not to leave the subject of the making of mead
without some mention of what is left of its culture in
the peasantry of England, among the cottagers, farmers, and
bee-masters.

We have seen how, through the combination of a variety
of causes, the chief of which were the steady increase in the
human population forcing the price of honey ever upwards,
and the Reformation which destroyed a ritual based upon
wax candles, the use of which had retarded the too rapid
decline of bee-keeping throughout the Middle Ages, there
took place a rapid declension in the manufacture of meads.

By the end of the eighteenth century the art of making
mead had passed entirely, or almost so, into the hands of
the peasantry, and what little of the craft has been maintained is due to their tenacity in holding to old customs and
ideas.

To-day the whole stage is set for a revival of mead-making,
and if that be so, the bridge between the heyday of the art
and its renaissance will be the meads of these country-folk.
Therefore, they deserve some comment for that reason alone.
While, by doing so, an opportunity will be provided for
describing the qualities of their meads and some of their
recipes.

In the east and south of England the mead has always been
given its English name, but from Warwickshire into the centre
of England, and reaching as far as the Thames it has tended
to be displaced by the Welsh word metheglin. Thus it is
that on the borders of Wessex we find the two terms meeting.
Thomas Hardy in his *Under the Greenwood Tree* tells us of the
householders of his beloved Wessex " bottling off old *mead* ",
and, again, in his *Tess* (II, 62, 1891) he writes—" I found the

123

mead . . . extremely alcoholic." While Gilbert White, writing on 12th December, 1775, from his Hampshire border village of Selborne, describes the idiot boy of the village whose whole propensity was towards bees, seeking them out, sucking the honey from them, and putting them between his shirt and his body, and behaving as a very *apiaster* or bee-bird. In the course of which description of this unfortunate youth, he tells of his sliding into the bee-gardens, and sitting before the hives, sometimes overturning them, in his passion for honey, and " where *metheglin* was making he would linger round the tubs and vessels, begging a draught of what he called bees' wine ".

Excepting, perhaps, for that mead which the late Reverend Tickner Edwardes describes from Sussex, that made by Brother Adam at Buckfast, and a very few others, most meads which are still made, despite the regional differences which would call them metheglins in the centre of England, and mead in the south and east, are really *spiced* sack-meads, or, in other words, sack-metheglins.

At this we ought not to be surprised. For we have seen how throughout the Middle Ages the tendency was to neglect the lighter and drier for the sweet and stronger mead, and finally with the coming of the Welsh Tudors the fashion for spiced liquor became general in England. With the result that, as the declension of mead occurred at that very time, the last impress left on the tradition of the craft was that of sack-metheglin rather than sack-mead or mead.

To make good mead, of excellent dryness, of little acid, and of robustness with fine flavour and good bouquet, is an extremely difficult and highly skilled accomplishment. The same thing is true of good wines, and that is why in wine-producing countries almost every farmer makes wine but only the specialists export their wines—because their wines alone are worthy of export, although the others are good enough for the less developed tastes and humbler uses of those who make them.

Therefore as one must not judge fine wine by that produced

by the peasant, so one must not expect too much of his meads.

The recipes which he follows, as we should expect, are not such as will produce a fine mead, sack-mead, or metheglin, as they are practical rule-of-thumb recipes such as the housewife can handle in the midst of her other duties, and they aim at producing with reasonable certainty a drinkable and not a " vintage " liquor.

Let us take a few of these cottage recipes, by way of example, which are typical of the metheglin type of mead, and we will see how strong and coarse they are by comparison with any drink of a pure character relying solely on the qualities of its honey, good vinting, and careful keeping and handling. It is of interest to note, too, that there is little doubt that the nearer we come to our own times, the worse are the recipes because they are further from the real wine in type.

One seventeenth-century cookery book [201] not only adds numerous and unnecessary herbs, but " well-bruised " ginger by the pound, juice of "lemmons", cinnamon, cloves, mace, nutmegs, and well-bruised juniper berries! Of course a highly spiced drink is the result but it is not mead—although it would be accepted as such by many honey shows in England to-day. It is, indeed, truly metheglin, a spiced drink.

Of a like nature are the following two recipes for a sack-metheglin, taken at random :

" Take of spring-water what quantity you please, and make it more than blood-warm, and dissolve honey in it till 'tis strong enough to bear an egg, the breadth of a shilling ; then boil it gently near an hour, taking off the scum as it rises ; then put to about nine or ten gallons seven or eight large blades of mace, three nutmegs quartered, twenty cloves, three or four sticks of cinnamon, two or three roots of ginger, and a quarter of an ounce of Jamaica pepper ; put these spices into the kettle to the honey and water, a whole lemon, with a sprig of sweet-briar and a sprig of rosemary ; tie the briar and rosemary together, and when they have boiled a little while take them out and throw them away ; but let your liquor stand on the spice in a clean earthen pot till the next day ; then strain it into a vessel that is fit for it ; put the spice in a bag, and

hang it in the vessel, stop it, and at three months draw it into bottles.
Be sure that 'tis fine when 'tis bottled ; after 'tis bottled six weeks
'tis fit to drink." [202]

.   .   .   .

" Mix the whites of six eggs with twelve gallons of spring-water :
add twenty pounds of the best virgin honey and the peeling of three
lemons ; boil it an hour, and then put into it some rosemary, cloves,
mace, and ginger ; when quite cold add a spoonful or two of yeast,
tun it, and when it has done working stop it up close. In a few
months bottle it off, and deposit in a cool cellar." [203]

.   .   .   .

When we come to an early nineteenth-century cookery
book we find that the degeneration has gone further. Now
hops, of all things, are added and, of course, a quart of
brandy ! [204]

Here we see the taste for sweetness, spirits, and hops com-
peting to make a mixture of all the prevailing English drinks,
and yet this mixture is called by the uninformed " mead ",
simply because honey is a basic ingredient. Just as the
original ale became contaminated with hops now we have
mead itself ruined by this pungent bitter herb. I have
sampled " mead " or metheglin made to one of these recipes
and the natural flavours of the honey which should provide
the bouquet have been completely destroyed.

To-day, despite the fact that the cost of spirits has made
it impossible to put several bottles of brandy into the cask,
there is no tax on hops and so they continue to be prescribed.
For instance, in an otherwise useful little book for the housewife,[205] we read that for every 2 lb. of fresh honey there is
to be 1 lb. of dried hops ! This, indeed, is nothing but a
strong hop beer made with honey instead of malt. Yet it is
what somebody believes to be mead.

Just before leaving for Sicily, when staying with Capt. B. S.
Townroe, at Yately, together we visited an old bee-master
who with pride showed his keg in which he made his " mead "
from the recipe given him by one of the biggest bee-masters
in southern England, and this, besides all or many of these
additions we have already mentioned, contained many pounds

of raisins ! Here we see the old mead partaking of a vinous character and so becoming somewhat of a pyment. But it is not and cannot be considered mead—no matter how good the resulting liquor may be.

To cover all these varied and mainly spiced drinks compounded with honey it would be as well to encourage either the spread of the Welsh name metheglin, which has already gained a fair currency, or else qualify the word mead with " spiced ", reserving the names of mead and sack-mead for specific meads whose qualities are easily definable. The honey shows certainly do not expect to get only mead, but rather metheglin for their entries, and, until their members and judges know, understand, and appreciate mead, they ought not to hold exhibitions of mead but of metheglin. There is certainly room in an age suffering an appalling lack of variety in its beverages, for all these sweet, spiced, and bitter drinks, but they ought not to be called mead, lest the gods rise up from Valhalla and confound us. It is to be hoped, however, that while they will be continued to be made, the quality of this metheglin will be improved by getting rid of all those unnecessary spicings, raisins, and the excessive quantities of sugar which have crept in, in ever-increasing quantities, from Tudor times onwards.

Besides such meads made upon the basis of wrong principles it is to be feared that much downright bad and undrinkable mead is made by many amateurs. This, in part, is to be understood, as wine-making is a skilled occupation, and the dangers of acetification are not inconsiderable. Nevertheless, a part of this badly made mead is due to completely wrong ideas and methods. What are we to say to a recipe for mead, given in *Bee Craft* (April, 1942, p. 35), which says—" Mead can be made from old combs—e.g. from a stock that has died in the winter, leaving some stores too messy to eat as honey and too mouldy for giving to the bees " ? How can such methods produce anything, as a general rule, but a richly acid liquor in which every type of wine disease will probably be found ?

It is the combination of lack of skill and such wrong advice and practices which accounts for the poor meads which are found to be the normal result of the amateur's efforts.

While criticizing the country-folks' brew and stating that, with few exceptions, it is not mead, and, even when properly made, is rather than mead an over-spiced and over-sweet sack-metheglin, it should be made clear that there is all honour to be paid to the housewives of these humble homes who through the ages have at least carried on, or have attempted to carry on, the tradition of making a mead.

Furthermore, let it be said without hesitation, when the country-folk (and any folk for that matter) can lay by sufficient provision out of their daily store, out of which they can succeed in making a keg, or some bottles, of any wine for the day of a festival, we have a people who are making strides in civilization. Unfortunately this is not generally the case to-day and has not been for nearly a century—Dr. Druit [206] complained in 1865 that whereas in his boyhood, in a part of ancient Wessex, a glass of " mead " could be had at the door of any better-class cottage, at the time of writing

" Bees are more scarce ; cottagers, if they keep them, sell their honey and buy beer ; but in all these matters *housewifery*, or the cost of keeping house comfortably, is dying out. Home-made and home-spun are displaced by manufactures and shoddy. Formerly, baker's bread or brewer's beer were despised as unworthy to be set by the side of the home-made . . . but the progress of events makes our whole population less housewifely, and more dependent on the shop."

Druit describes a condition that is much further developed to-day than in his days, and difficult as he may have found it to gather together bottles of mead or metheglin it would have been well-nigh impossible before the war of 1939–45. He, fortunately, describes these bottles of honey-wine for us, and although it is clear that most of them were of the coarser metheglin type, ill-made and highly spiced with hops no doubt, some still seem to have been well-made meads and metheglins. But all of them were of the sack character.

Some of his remarks are worth quoting, coming as they do from a man who was a wine-lover and still fairly familiar with various types of mead.

Of the bad sort of sack-mead and sack-metheglin we have : [207]

(1) " A specimen about five years old, vilely made, full of un-fermented honey . . . very sweet . . . alcoholic strength 18."

(2) And " from a cottage on Pool Heath, made 1864 ; bad condition, actively fermenting, acid, sweet and heady . . . alcoholic strength 23 ".[208]

These examples were bad partly because of being ill-made and ill-kept and perhaps also through the adulterants to which we have referred.

On the other hand, listen to what he says about a well-made sack-mead.[209]

" A magnificent specimen from an eminent tradesman at Christchurch, Hants., made in 1814 and consequently more than fifty years old ; . . . alcoholic strength 16. Marvellously soft, full flavoured and fragrant ; a little drop perfumes a glass so that it is difficult to wash off."

In fine, Druit [210] says that in his experience a good (sack-) mead is nearly dry, i.e. not sweet, and by age " it acquires a remarkably luscious perfume like that of Tokay ".

If the unskilled householder could occasionally on the hit-and-miss principle achieve such a sack-mead it serves to show what could consistently be obtained as knowledge of the true art of meading became spread once more throughout the country.

Of what can be achieved in the way of mead liquors will be set out in a later chapter in a brief review of the qualities of the various types of mead.

CHAPTER XII

THE GRAPE AND HONEY COMPARED

THIS chapter, in the very nature of the case, must only be
a short note upon the properties which go to make wine
and those which belong to honey and so are the basis of the
ancient Aryan drink of mead, and which will be found in
greater or lesser degree in all those other honey liquors which
we have discussed.

In the grape juice from which wine is made there is about
80 per cent water, and about 15 per cent grape sugar by
weight. But the latter varies from season to season, and is
greater in the south of Europe than in the north. In addition,
in fresh grapes there is a large amount of saccharomycetes,
and these are the natural yeasts in the juice of the grape.

By the action of this natural yeast the grape sugar in the
fermenting liquid (*must*) is split into ethyl alcohol and carbon
dioxide. After fermentation is complete the grape sugar has
disappeared, or almost so, and in its place we have ethyl
alcohol and carbon dioxide.

Besides grape sugar (which with the water forms about
95 per cent of the total juice by weight) there is a large
variety of acids and other substances which are there in
very small parts and yet are most important in the making
of the wine.

Among these are mineral acids drawn from the soil in
which the grape was grown as well as oils from the pips, acids
from the stalks, and cellulose from the skins and so on. Fermentation, however, causes the appearance of entirely new
things in the liquid, and among these are glycerine, alcohols
of a different nature to ethyl alcohol, some acids, aldehydes
and esters. But all of these are only a small proportion of
the whole.

From these wine is made, in the still wines the carbon

dioxide being permitted to escape. From the esters and a proper balancing of the right acids, we get the bouquet which marks out a fine wine, in which there is a proper balance of sugar and acidity.

Certain wines are fortified by brandy or spirit which should be distilled from wine—but, often, in some of the cheapest wines, is not and comes from less desirable sources. Fortification, in moderation and made from sound wine and good mature spirit, when it improves the wine can be justified —and there is little doubt that in northern climates where the cold requires a warming effect the wine so treated is very comforting. Indeed, it may even be argued that taken in moderation, it is beneficial to a meat-eating population, such as we were once in days before rationing, which requires such aids to the digestion. But, at the same time, it cannot be denied that it is the spirit element in Port and Sherry which makes them injurious to sufferers from neuritis and gout and not the wine itself. Pyment and hippocras types of liquors when fortified, which is not always the case, really fall into the same categories as Port although of a different bouquet and flavour.

In contrast with the grape, honey contains a large amount of the fruit sugar called fructose or laevulose. In honey it amounts to as much as 40 per cent or thereabouts by weight, while in the grape it is very much less (about 15%).

This sugar is often prescribed for diabetics in place of the cane sugar (sucrose).[211] In that process of chemical change in the living cell of the human body called metabolism, this sugar is associated with the formation of tissues.

Like the grape, on the other hand, honey has grape sugar (dextrose). It amounts to about 34 per cent. In metabolism this sugar is connected with respiration.

Naturally, the proportions of these two sugars, as well as of the other constituents of honey, vary from one to another. For instance, fructose (laevulose) sugar is found in greater proportion in dark honey than in the lighter varieties. Such honeys, as a consequence, flow more freely than the lighter types in which dextrose (grape sugar or glucose) is in a larger proportion.   Despite this variation between one honey and another, these figures, for all that, can be taken as fairly typical of honey as a whole.

In addition to these two invert sugars honey has a very small element, amounting to about 1·9 per cent only, of ordinary cane or sucrose sugar.

However, honey consists of much more than mere sugars, important as these are.   Honey is the product which the bee has manufactured from the nectar of the flowers and blossoms, and, consequently, it contains substances derived from them. For instance, there are aromatic oils, essences, gums and resins, and valuable assimilable salts, such as those of iron, phosphorus, lime, sodium, potassium, sulphur, and manganese.   Of these minerals, 1 lb. of honey has in it 21 per cent of the daily requirement of iron and 5 per cent of that of phosphorus.[212]   Besides these there are dextrine, albumin, waxes, fats, formic and malic acids, and complex digestive enzymes, which convert the small quantity of cane sugar into the grape and fruit sugars.[213]   The quantities of these are, as may be expected, in many cases very small, but they are extremely important in the composition of honey for all that.   The dextrines and gums amount to about 1·5 per cent, the salts mentioned to 0·2 per cent, and the ash to about 0·15 per cent.

Vitamins, A, B, C, and K are found in honey,[214] but they are sometimes, in commercially produced honey, of no significance, the amounts being usually very small owing to over-filtration.   The vitamins would appear to be associated with the pollen, and as it is the purpose of the bee-keeper to keep the pollen granules out of his extracted honey, the chance of vitamins occurring in too finely strained honey is small.   On the other hand there are presumably more in the honey-*must* used in mead-making, but what happens to vitamins in the process of fermentation the writer does not know.

Honey is particularly valuable because of the large amount

of dextrose and laevulose sugars which it contains, as these, unlike the ordinary cane sugar which unhappily enters into so much of our modern diet, are readily absorbed by the human being. Cane sugar is not easily assimilated, and has to undergo chemical changes, which generate gases, for instance, before it can be consumed.

The value of these sugars of the honey is seen in the case of ulcers of the stomach, which it has been known for a long time can be cured by the use of honey, and for which it has been tried recently in a very thorough and effective manner in Russian clinics. In cases of malnutrition, especially that of children, and in typhoid fever and liver troubles it has been found of great benefit.[215] Tickner Edwardes [216] reminds us that in all wasting diseases, and particularly in consumption, honey is one of the most beneficial builders up of the patient.

Beck and Smedley, in their work, *Honey and Your Health* (London, 1947, pp. 31–39) point to an interesting series of medical facts connected with honey. For instance, medical research has shown that honey is the best of all foods for raising the blood level. While in Austria it has been proved that the haemoglobin (blood count) has been increased $8\frac{1}{2}$ per cent by one year's diet of 2 tablespoons of honey daily. They point out that the Vitamin K in honey is of considerable value in matters of haemorrhage.

According to the same authors honey has the power to destroy bacteria, and this would account for its use in surgery, where it can be used in much the same way as one would employ tincture of iodine.

According to Professor Adamkiewiecz honey is important in maintaining the strength and rhythm of the heart.[217] Alin Caillas, a French investigator, stresses the importance of honey because of its calcium and salts of phosphorus, especially for overworked and weak nerves.[218] While others have seen in honey radio-active properties of a curative nature.[219]

Whatever truth there may be in these, this much at least can be said, that both the grape and the honeycomb are produced in the heats of summer, and if any articles of food, and in this case of drink, can confer benefits, from sunlight and sun heat, to those who partake of them, it is surely wine and mead.

The calories contained in one pound of honey amount to 1,450 to 1,480, which is between 50 and 80 more calories than those allowed to us by our daily food ration in post-war Britain ! [220] Put another way, one pound of honey is equal to 43 per cent of the normal daily requirement. [221] The importance of honey as a concentrated food is perhaps most forcibly expressed by saying that in nourishment value one pound of honey is equal to three pounds of meat. [222] This would certainly seem to justify the German saying we have already quoted—that mead (or honey) is as strong as meat !

It would also support the belief of the ancient Greeks who held that honey was an important ingredient in any diet—intended to increase the vital powers and prolong life. On such honey diets Pythagoras lived to 90 years of life, Appolonius to 113, Anacreon to 115, and Democritus to 109. Hippocrates, the father of medicine, certainly prescribed honey for all those who wished to enjoy a long life. We know that the same belief existed among the Romans, for we find Pliny the Elder pointing to the inhabitants of certain bee-keeping areas as examples of people of long life.

Malic acid, a constituent of cider, is said to be the element which counteracts gout and rheumatism. Certainly sufferers from gout seem to be able to drink cider when they cannot touch wine, beer, or spirits. As malic is the acid found in honey, we may assume that mead either has the same effect as cider, or, if not, at any rate, the basic malic acid must go far to counteract the bad effects of the alcohol on gout sufferers.

It is worth quoting in this connection Beck and Smedley concerning the qualities of mead :

" For many centuries mead was considered a veritable ' elixir vitae '. Its principal medicinal value was in kidney ailments, as an excellent diuretic without disastrous effects upon the kidneys. As for gout and rheumatism, mead ranked not only as a curative but also as a preventive medicine. It was widely used as a good digestive and laxative." [223]

Now all these qualities of honey undergo change and modification under the processes of fermentation, just as the original qualities of the grape do likewise, but it is, nevertheless, obvious that mead, taking up into itself so many things which are of themselves of such prime importance to the well-being of the human being, must be a liquor of outstanding merit.

It is, consequently, not surprising that the ancients held firmly to the belief in the powers of mead, some of which we have necessarily had to discuss when going over the conceptions which they envisaged attached themselves to the *nectar* of the gods. Those views of ancient men, based upon a general rule-of-thumb assessment of experience, accumulated through the ages, were evidently not far from the truth. Its strengthening and vitalizing quality, its food value, its power to heal, all these are to be found in their conceptions of mead, quite apart from other qualities attributed to it, which are more particularly associated with the alcoholic stimulation of the liquor, such as its gift of tongues, and poetry.

In short, all knowledge, ancient and modern, witnesses to the stimulating, curative, restorative, and aphrodisiac qualities of this liquor.

In this last connection it might be pointed out that this claim for mead is much more surely grounded than the extravagant claims which have been made for a certain Cyprian wine [224] sold at exorbitant prices in tiny glasses in Venice and Paris. Of course that wine, and probably others, too, share this characteristic in some measure, in so far as wine of itself is a liquor very close in type to mead. But these properties are peculiarly those of mead rather than of wine.

Although having nothing to do with the relative characteristics of grape juice and honey respectively, it is not inappropriate here to refer to the mode of manufacture of the two liquors since this raises a question of hygiene not unimportant in these enlightened days. What is now to be said may not be applicable to all wine, but, nevertheless, it is, in whole or part, true of most of them, and therefore criticism is, in a large number of instances, quite justified.

The honey for the manufacture of mead, in common with all honey produced, is extracted from the combs cleanly and hygienically. It is not handled by men as grapes have to be. Instead, in bee- and fly-proof rooms, it is poured into containers, from which, in due course, it is run into vats along with the appropriate ferments, and the right quantity of water, and, in its proper time, without any further handling whatever, and, indeed, without even seeing the light of day, it becomes mead, sack-mead, metheglin, or whatever other mead liquor is intended.

All this stands out in sharp contrast to the treatment which the grape receives.

First the grapes must be picked, and packed into panniers, picked over in the heat and dust of the warm summer days for broken and rotting fruit, and then carried to the presses. There the juice is squeezed from the grapes, and this is as often as not done by the traditional method of treading the grapes.

Charles Tovey describes the treading of the grapes at the Château Margaux, where everything was neat and tidy, as it should be in any wine- or mead-making establishment—but, nevertheless, the work was done with the bare feet. His description of the treading of the grapes in a Portuguese vineyard, where, in all probability everything was much more primitive is—

" When the trough or lager is filled with grapes, a ' gang ' of men jump in, and forming a close line with their arms on each other's shoulders, advance and retire with measured step, treading the fruit to the sound of bagpipe, the drum, and the fife." [225]

In some vineyards the vigneron himself goes in up to his neck. It is true that this is after being soaped and hosed, but even these precautions do not make the process any the more attractive.

No doubt about the picturesqueness of such methods, of which this drab life is all too bereft in these days, but, when all is said and done, it is not an ideal method of handling liquor which men are going to drink. Yet it is a well-nigh universal practice. Indeed, we remember arguing once with the *Sindaco* (Mayor) of Palermo over dinner on this very point, and he swore by the efficacy of the feet in treading the grapes, as though good wine could not be produced in any other way. One can well imagine, in the more primitive vineyards, that the philosophy of some of the old-fashioned cider-makers still holds good, when they used to say about impurities trodden into the liquor from the farmyard—" It doan't matter, Maister, the muck all comes off in the scum ! "

This is, nevertheless, not all that might be said upon this subject. It is hard to escape the memory of the ever-hovering cloud of flies, or, in Greece, and some other countries too, the traditional adulterants, such as pitch, turpentine, gypsum, and salt, added to the juice, no doubt, at first to prevent the deterioration of the liquor because of the introduction of so many impurities.

To say all this may appear to be an attack upon wine. It is not intended to be such. These scenes of perspiring men and women carrying the panniers to the press, of men pressing the grapes empurpled to the knees, and of the flies feeding on all juice, skins, and *must* they can light upon, will no more prevent one from drinking a good wine, no more than the housewife will refuse to use the tomato ketchups and concentrates prepared in like climates under conditions which, in the very nature of the circumstances, are far from desirable. Furthermore, nature has her own way in dealing with too much contamination, by turning the wine bad : and there is an end of it. Consequently it is only the best that can live to be classified as good wine. As a result, despite all that has been said, these thoughts ought not to deter anyone from drinking a glass of wine.

Nevertheless, mead needs no such apology in connection with its preparation.   In an age so acutely conscious of the need for hygiene, this is a decided gain—and comfort too. It is a quality in mead which must be added to that already lengthy list of characteristics which go to justify the claims made for it both by tradition and more modern scientific evaluation.

No words which one can write can adequately describe the fine qualities of a good wine, and this is even more true for mead, combining as it does the scent of subtle essences and nectars from a thousand blossoms of field and woodland, in its clear, sparkling, light yellow liquid.   Such a drink, subtle of flavour and delicate of aroma, well justifies the old English belief that it was served in heaven.

" Let Sybaris' well spring honey for me, and ere the sun is up
May the wench that goes for water draw honeycombs for my cup."
(Theocritus, *The Goatherd and the Shepherd*, 126 -7.)

CHAPTER XIII

HORKS, MAZERS AND METHER CUPS

A NY study of mead must, of necessity, make some acquaintance with the drinking vessels out of which this ancient drink was quaffed. It is, therefore, of interest to make a brief mention of these. The more so is this the case since it is fortunate that we know of a traditional association of mead with two types of old drinking vessels, the Mazer cup and the Mether cup.

Before treating of these two forms of drinking vessels out of which we know mead was drunk, it is as well to discuss them with all the drinking vessels used by our ancestors, so that we may have their correct setting.

Perhaps the oldest of vessels were the drinking horns, and although these were at first, no doubt, of plain horn, at a very early period they became highly ornamented with silver, gold, and silver gilt—for our prehistoric Aryan ancestors had advanced a long way in the technical arts. Out of them ale, wine, as well as mead, were drunk.

Julius Caesar [226] observed this decoration of the drinking horns among the ancient Germans, for he says that they preserved the horns of buffaloes " with great care, tip their edges with silver and use them instead of cups on their most solemn festivals ".

Drinking horns are frequently mentioned in the Welsh bards as in use at the banquets and here too they are decorated with silver. We read thus, in the poem by Owain Kyveiliog, Prince of Powis, whose drinking horn was called Hirlas :

> " The highly honoured buffalo-horn Hirlas,
> enriched with ancient silver." [227]

In the *Heimskringla* we read of the same fashion of decoration in connection with the magnificence of King Harold—

" While King Harold and his men had entirely new vessels and horns adorned with gold, all with carved figures and shining like glass." [228]   These were presumably of buffalo horn, but we also find deer horn cups mentioned in the *Heimskringla* as well.[229]

The Niebelungen heroes quaffed their mead also from such ox-horns as well as from golden goblets.

We learn too that King Witlaf of Mercia gave such a horn from his table to the Abbey of Crowland, so that the senior brethren should drink from it on high festivals, and, in doing so, remember the soul of the giver.

Cambden figures a magnificent example of one of these old horns (called the Charter Horn) from Kilkenny, Ireland.[230] Perhaps one of the finest horns is the horn of the Danish lord Ulf, which has fortunately survived and is now in York Minster, where it lies as token of the gift of his lands to the Minster.

Such drinking horns lasted on in use till after the Norman Conquest, not because of their convenience (for they are the most awkward vessels ever devised) but because of the traditional symbolism associated with them, which as early as Caesar's time made them the fitting cups for solemn festivals. As a horn cannot be put down until it is drained, the guest was given every hospitality by having a full horn of mead or ale which he had to finish.

Apparently, the symbol of the mead-horn was used by our ancestors for Christmas, or the Yule-tide, since an ancient runic calendar has been found in Scandinavia which shows these horns for this period of the year. (Incidentally, September is typified by a beehive and a swarm of bees—the harvest of the raw material for the mead symbolizing all harvest-tide.)

But, horns were not the sole drinking vessels—on the contrary, the bowl was more normal. Originally it must have been made solely of wood. But later it became ornamented with silver and ultimately we read of silver cups.

The wooden vessels, whether ornamented with silver or not,

are known as mazers, from a Middle English word related to maple, which was the favourite wood for this vessel. The Icelandic word *mösurr*, which is obviously the same as mazer, means a maple-tree. The old French is *maselin* and in that form we find it in Chaucer. The old Germanic word *másá* means a spot, and it has been suggested that the spotted nature of the grain of maple wood led to this name.[231] But we find that they were made of other woods as well. There is an old one of the thirteenth century thought to be of ash.[232] We read in the *Heimskringla* of one of birch, as we shall see below. While Rabelais [233] talks of " eyes as red as a mazer made of an alder tree " in allusion to the knots, or eyes, in the polished wood of the bowl. In an old North Country and Midlands wassail song, we hear of a mazer made of rosemary—" our wassail cup is made of rosemary-tree ".[234]

The mazer, therefore, being a wooden cup, must go back to very primitive times. It was already old when Theocritus wrote—" but I'll give you a fine great mazer to boot, well scoured with sweet beeswax, and of two lugs, bran-span-new and the smack of the graver upon it yet ".[235]

We read frequently of bowls in *Beowulf* and the *Heimskringla*, but whether these were truly mazers is not clear. There is, however, an obvious allusion to a mazer, but one of a less common form than usual in that it had a handle, and so was somewhat like the mazer of Theocritus, in the *Heimskringla* :

" King Harold gave Tore of Steig at that feast a bowl of mountain birch, that was encircled with a silver ring, and had a silver handle, both which parts were gilt." [236]

A few examples of these handled mazers, which were still in use in the Middle Ages, have survived to the present day.

Much earlier than this the bowls of wood had been copied in silver and gold, and, as, in time, the wooden bowls began to be put on metal bases, so we find the metal bowls developing in a parallel fashion, until, at a later period, the bowl, whether of wood or metal, was mounted on a silver stem.

How far these early mazers and cups were mounted on
stems is doubtful, but probably very few of them were.   They
would seem from old illustrations, the Bayeux tapestry for
instance, to have been mainly bowls rather than cups or
goblets.

The *Heimskringla*, again, has many references to such table
cups of wood or metal or both.   For instance :

" King Olaf used the fashion, which was introduced from the
courts of foreign kings, of letting his grand-butler stand at the end
of the table, and fill the table-cups for himself and the other distinguished guests who sat at the table." [237]

Here we do not know what was the material of the vessel,
but in this next entry the cup was of silver :

" King Granmar told his daughter Hildigunn, who was a remarkably beautiful girl, to make ready to carry ale to the Vikings.   There
upon she took a silver goblet, filled it, bowed before King Hjorvard,
and said ' Success to all Ylfinger : this cup to the memory of Rolf
Krake '—and drank out the half and handed the cup to King
Hjorvard." [238]

From the following account we have another case of a
valuable metal cup :

" The treasurer replies, ' Sire, as far as I know, all articles of any
value are given away.'
The King : ' Here is a drinking goblet remaining ; take this,
bishop, it is not without value.' " [239]

As the bishop made this cup into a chalice on arriving in
Iceland, it suggests that from a very early period the church
tended to have its own distinctive forms of cups for chalices.
The difference, apart from other features of ecclesiastical
significance, was probably that the secular cup tended to
follow the form of the mazer, and had a wide low bowl instead
of a high narrow one.

Among the Anglo-Saxons there appears to have been a mass
of silver vessels.   We find, for instance, that Byrhtric in his
will bequeathed three silver cups, while Wulfur bequeathed
four cups, two of which he described as of £4 value.   The
Lady Ethelgwa gave two such cups to the Abbey of Ramsey

for use in the refectory, so that the monks, when drinking therefrom, should bear her in remembrance. We also read that Wynfleda gave besides four silver cups, a cup with a

Fig. 8

An Angel Dining

Sketched from an old Oxford MS. depicting by St. Cuthbert entertaining an Angel at Ripon.
Note the Mazers on the table

fringed edge, a wooden cup variegated with gold, a wooden knobbed cup, and two *smicere scencing cuppan*, or very handsome drinking cups. In other places we read of a gold cup and gold dish, a gold cup of immense weight, and so on.[240]

The wooden cup variegated with gold, and a wooden knobbed cup sound very like a mazer.

We read of a king in 833 giving away his gilt cup, engraved without with vine-dressers fighting a dragon, which he called his " cross-bowl " because it had a cross marked within it.[241] At an early date a boss of metal was placed in the centre of the wooden mazer bowls, presumably to protect the weakest part of the wood. This became known as the " print " and it was usually ornamented by engraving or enamelling. Can we have here then, another mazer ?

In *Beowulf* there are possibly references to mazers where we read of plated bowls :

" Or polisheth | the plated bowl,
The drinking-cup dear." [242]

Fortunately we have surviving the account of an Anglo-Saxon mazer—that of the Venerable Bede himself, which was to be found in the Frater House at Durham, and which had received later additions (as mazers did in the course of their change in form from age to age) by the way of being lined inside with silver double-gilt, although the outside remained of black maple, and by silver straps down the outside.[243] Another mazer of a great ecclesiastic which had received additions in a like manner was that of Thomas of Canterbury who died in 1170, and it is mentioned in an inventory of 1315 of Christchurch Priory as " the cup of St. Thomas, silver and gilt inside, with a foot added to it ".[244]

Luckily many mazers have come down to us, according to Sir Charles Jackson,[245] as many as sixty have survived the ravages of time.

Some of these mazers are of the large communal type, and among these are :

The Scrope mazer bowl. This is lined inside with silver, and in the centre of this silver lining there is a much raised and richly embossed shield of arms of the York Cordwainers.[246]

This mazer is a bowl and not placed upon a stem. The Scrope mazer is not a small cup like those of the monks of

Durham, which were for individual use, but is over one foot across, and is a common " grace cup ", used for a ceremonial drinking together from the same bowl—a symbol of fellowship common with our ancestors.

The Rochester mazer, like the Scrope mazer, is a large one, and not upon a stem, dating from somewhere about 1532–33, and now in the British Museum.

The Bannatyne or Bute mazer [247] is one of the finest of these large mazer bowls for common " grace cup " purposes.

PLATE I

The Bannatyne or Bute Mazer

An example of the Mazer in the form of a bowl. The rim, base, and side strips are of silver and the bowl is of wood

We sometimes read in old wills of such large mazers as these Bannatyne, Rochester, and Scrope mazers. For example, in the will of Cristofer Stapulton of Wyghall Esquyer dated 1537 we read of " one greete holoe boole, gilt with a cover ".[248]

Throughout the Middle Ages the mazer was the most common drinking vessel, often being richly ornamented with silver gilt both without and at times within, with an enamelled or engraved medallion inside, sometimes having highly ornamented covers, and on occasions long stems or feet in the case of the individual mazers.

We may well realize how common these cups were when

we learn that each monk at Durham had to have his own
mazer.[249]

Any examination of old wills provides frequent references
to mazers being bequeathed as valuable possessions.

For example, in the registers at Carlisle [250] for the fourteenth
century we read of :

27th July 1362 to Dom. John of Wylton 2 mazers (with a dun
hackney horse, sheep and calves).

2nd Feb. 1353/4. To Dom John of Penrith, Canon, a surplice and
a little mazer cup.

29th Sept. 1357. To the brothers [of the Minor Friars] my mazer
worth 14 shillings [and] to John Boon my little mazer and my
chafing dish [? *caminum igneum*] and sword, and dinner table
along with the bands of rich embroidery belonging to my
ecclesiastical vestments.

20th March 1357. To the Carmelite brothers of Appelby my large
mazer and to Lady Isabelle de Clifford, wife of Lord Thomas
de Musgrave my little mazer.

18th Oct. 1362. To Lady Margaret de Malton, a maze cup.

Old literature makes frequent references to the mazer. For
instance, in the Scottish Ballad of Gil Morrice we find :

> " Then up an spake the bauld baron,
> An angry man was hee ;
> He's tain the table wi' his foot,
> Sae has he wi' his knee ;
> *Till siller cup and mazer dish*
> In flinders he gard flee." [251]

While Spenser wrote :

> " A mazer ywrought of the maple wood
> Whereon is enchased many a fair sight
> Of bears and tigers than man fierce war." [252]

As late as Jacobean times it was still a vessel in common
use. Thus we find in the ballad, " The Man in the Moon
drinks Claret ", sung at the Curtain Theatre, Shoreditch, 1610,
the opening lines :

> " Bacchus, the father of drunken nowles,
> Full *mazers*, beakers, glasses, bowls." [253]

The mazer sometimes appeared as a service in legal tenures.
For we find that the Manor of Bilsington Inferior was held

at the time of Edward III by service of three maple cups at the King's Coronation, and this particular service was continued till as late as the time of George III.[254]

Yet knowledge is lost so readily and completely that there are this day in England few who know what is a mazer. There are three stages in the development of the mazer in the Middle Ages. From the fourteenth to fifteenth centuries the bowls were generally deep, with plain, narrow, silver bands. From the middle of the fifteenth century to the middle of the sixteenth century the bowls became shallower. In the succeeding Elizabethan period metal straps connecting the band round the rim to the foot were often added.

As a development from the simple small bowl made for individual use, as against the large bowl used as a " grace cup " like the Scrope or Bannatyne mazer, came the types of mazers surviving at Pembroke and Corpus Christi Colleges at Cambridge and All Souls at Oxford, which are characterized by a stem. These are, in form, the forerunners of the metal goblets or cups.

This type of mazer on a stem is found in Scotland in several interesting surviving pieces, but these are so big (with a diameter of about 8 inches for the bowls) that they almost belong to the large communal series, rather than the individual cup. But their form is much the same as in the smaller mazers. Among these old Scottish cups are the St. Mary's mazer,[255] the Ferguson mazer (sixteenth century), the Tulloch mazer (1557 or thereabouts) and the St. Leonard's " mazer ", which is probably early seventeenth century and is made entirely of silver.[256]

Here, in the mazer cup, we have the old English drinking vessel of the Middle Ages, which reached back on the one hand into far antiquity and on the other lasted on to the Elizabethans, and the early Stuarts, and which is still occasionally made by silversmiths.[257] From the mazer form developed the famous Tudor cup of 1523, and a whole range of silver cups. Out of the mazer was undoubtedly drunk all manner of wines, but, because of the position of mead in

Old English society it is obvious that the mazer must often have been the normal vessel to hold it. Chaucer certainly treated it as a natural cup in which to serve his mead when he wrote :

> " They sette him first the sweete wyn
> And mede eek in a mazelyn." [258]

PLATE II

An Example of a Standing Mazer Cup

The bowl is of wood, and the stem and rim is of silver

In whatever they set the sweet wine before Sir Thopas, this leaves no doubt that the mead was served in a mazer.

Another quotation occurs which suggests the use of the mazer for mead, and that is from Pepys. He went to see an alms-house and had some " of their drink " (the use of which term gives the impression it was not wine and so quite likely mead) in a bowl type of mazer. He writes :

27th February, 1659/60.
" Up by four o'clock . . . to Saffron Walden, where at the White Hart we set up our horses . . . my landlord carried us through a very old hospital or almshouse, where forty poor people were maintained ; a very old foundation. . . . They brought me a draft of their drink in a brown bowl, tipt with silver, which I drank off, and at the bottom was a picture of the Virgin with the child in her arms, done in silver."

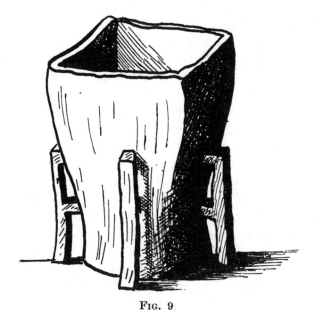

Fig. 9

Mether Cup
(After G. Clinch, *Handbook of English Antiquities*)

Besides the mazer which was certainly used for mead (whatever else it was used for) we have the mether cup which was used solely for mead.

Like the mazer it was made of wood, but the name is derived from the old form of the word for mead—meth. They are usually four-sided at the top and circular or oval at the bottom. They have a number of handles, varying from one to four, and they are placed at the foot, sometimes projecting below the bottom to form feet as well as handles. Their height varies from 6 to 12 inches and in capacity from about one to three pints! [259]

In my possession I have a rare one in Hedingham-ware pottery with four feet. Bingham, the Hedingham potter, always reproduced old forms, but whether he copied this from an earlier wooden or pottery form is not clear—although the latter is more likely. This specimen is $5\frac{3}{4}$ inches high.

But we ought not to overlook a curious note to a passage in Bohn's edition of Rabelais [260] as a comment upon the sentence—" He also told us that there was a phial of Sanc-Grael, a most divine thing, and known to a few." This note says that the " Sang-real " (royal blood) was a pretended relic of Christ's blood preserved by Joseph of Arimathea, when he washed the Saviour's body before he embalmed it. Whereas the Saint Graal, another relic, " is the precious dish in which the paschal lamb was served up which our Saviour ate with his disciples the eve of his death. *Graal is properly a bowl or mazer of potter's clay.*"

This note would suggest that mazers, and if so we may assume mether cups also, were sometimes made of pottery.

In passing, one may add an inference of some importance which comes out from an examination of these mether cups. If mead were normally in olden times the sweeter, sack-mead drink we should not expect a cup varying from one to three pints! Even for mead a cup holding up to three pints, the contents of seven champagne goblets, is quite a formidable proposition. Only a Falstaff could have managed so large a cup brimful of sack-mead or sack-metheglin.

Incidentally, small silver mether cups varying from three to four handles are made by the silversmiths. These are only about $2\frac{1}{2}$ inches high. Whether they are actual reproductions of a smaller variety or miniatures I do not know.

The mazer, now lined and mounted in silver as well as plain, gradually gave way, after the Elizabethan age, to the silver cup, although it has never ceased to be made in one form or another, and deserves to be revived because of its sheer beauty and the fullness of its character. The British became as noted for their silver wine goblets, many of which followed the mazer-form, as they had been for their mazers,

Fig. 10

Mether Cup in Hedingham-ware Pottery

until ignorance growing apace, a silver cup is now something which is made in any shape and size, but that suitable for liquor, and looked upon as a " trophy " for a mantelpiece, instead of being a useful and ornamental garnishing of the table. But up to the eighteenth century, as the following

quotation will show, if not much later, silver was in regular
use, "in the honest old scripture stile", as it still is for beer
in University colleges.

Letter to the Hon. Chas. Ross, Esq., of Balnagown, by Dun. Forbes,
Bunchrue, 9th May 1722.

DEAR SIR,
Your epistle from Fortrose found me in the company of no other
ladys than the imaginary nymphs and naiads that inhabite silvan
schens [scenes ?]   As our correspondence has been now a great while
interrupted you may believe I was very happy in the hopes of possessing them for some days without the impertinent interposition of
claret or your toast.   But whilst I was hugging myself in this fond
imagination The Provost appeared, and tho he pretended to comply
with the Rules of the Place as not to call for a glass, yet he cust the
generall's health at me in a great silver mugg ful of wine which he
calls drinking a cup to one's friend in the honest old Scripture
stile." 261

In all the aesthetics of drinking, the vessel from which the
liquor is drained is of no small importance, and many writers
upon wine have not failed to lay proper stress upon this fact.

But the learned wine-drinker has one great experience still
to come, when he holds in his hands the mazer, and, from its
open silver bowl and rim, sees the clear golden mead, shot
through with every reflected light within the room, bubbling
and dancing upwards, and, bursting upon the surface, breath-
ing forth its fleeting scent and bouquet.

The poet has yet to describe " mead eek in a mazelyn " but
in default of that description we might do worse than to take
John Fletecher's (1579–1625) of red wine in the mazer :

> " God Lyaeus, ever young,
> Ever honour'd, ever sung,
> Stain'd with blood of lusty grapes,
> In a thousand lusty shapes
> Dance upon the mazer's brim,
> In the crimson liquor swim ;
> From thy plenteous hand divine
> Let a river run with wine :
>   God of youth, let this day here
>   Enter neither care nor fear."

CHAPTER XIV

A BRIEF ACCOUNT OF THE QUALITIES OF MEAD

FROM what has been said the reader must have formed a fairly comprehensive general idea of the qualities of the various mead liquors which have been discussed in this book. But as there are wide variations, as indeed there must be, for the honey produces every range of white wine of which the grape is capable, it is as well to set out a brief account, somewhat of a synoptic table, which research, as well as the making of mead, teaches us are the general qualities of the various types of meads. Although, just as the grape varies from one type of grape to another, and from district to district, so does honey, and so it will be found that even meads which fall within the same class will vary one from another according to the race of the bee [262] and flowers from which the honey of which they are made comes. A second reason why there is some purpose in reviewing the qualities of the various meads is to attempt to establish a more precise definition of the types. For we have observed how through the ages there has been a shift, from time to time, of the exact meaning of the various names used for these liquors, and it is as well to bring to an end a condition of nomenclature so full of contradictions and fruitful of confusion.

Therefore, to our synopsis :

Mead is the general name for all drinks made of honey. But besides being a generalized name, it has now come to refer in a specialized sense, to that form of mead which is of a lower alcoholic strength (usually about 11 or 12 per cent), and of slight sweetness.

This mead may be still or sparkling, as, for that matter, can all wines, although some do not lend themselves to that treatment, no more than would a sack-mead or a sack-metheglin. Unless artificially stimulated during fermentation, mead, in the southern English climate at any rate, tends to be of slow fermentation when made from its own ferments. This leads to the production of an excellent liquor for it is a known fact that in all wine-making slow fermentation produces the highest grades of liquors.   Unfortunately this slow fermentation throws it open to many maladies, and that is no doubt why all the cottage recipes rely upon the introduction of yeast which tends to give a rapid fermentation : but that is done at some expense of the ultimate quality of the mead.

The bouquet of mead brings it near to that group of French white wines represented by the Moselles, although, at times it comes near to the drier Sauternes.   Like these wines it can range from a dry sweet to a dry wine, according to the original sugar content in the *must*, to the development of its age, and for the degree of fermentation.   However, if made too sweet, it falls into the next class.   Unless very old there is always a good body in mead, and its bouquet arises from the essences of the flowers, of which the original honey is composed, which are changed and developed by the processes of fermentation. The sparkling variety of mead tends to be a little lighter, as might be expected, than the still variety.   Both are good drinks, suitable for use wherever white wines are served at dinner.   The drier and sparkling varieties serving well for the earlier stages of the meal, and the richer and slightly sweet meads towards the close.   Mead therefore serves the same purposes for which we use Champagne, Moselle, Hock, Graves and Sauternes, according to its type and quality, and it should be served cold.

Sack-mead.   Sack-mead, again, according to age and strength, can vary from a full-bodied, strong liquor of a sweet character, to one of relatively fair dryness, as a result of good fermentation and keeping.   Because it is made from a greater strength of honey than is mead, as we should expect, those qualities which are peculiar to the honey are increased considerably, as is also the body, and the general " oiliness " of the liquor is clearly seen upon the glass or the silver of the mazer.

In the sweeter kinds of sack-mead we have a drink not unlike Imperial Tokay, that great Hungarian sweet wine, whose fragrance and quality is so greatly praised. Curiously enough, not only does Tokay resemble the sweeter sack-meads in sweetness and flavour, but it has many of the other, and more subtle elements, of sack-mead, including the same, or nearly the same, nutritional and medicinal qualities. For Tokay is often prescribed for debilitated people when all the other remedies known to medicine have been abandoned. In this respect, Tokay is a rival of, and, since mead is the older drink, unconscious imitation of, sack-mead. Tokay, and several other of the best Hungarian wines (such as dry Ruszte), retain an almost floral fragrance, and this fragrance, naturally, is an especial quality of sack-mead. It would seem as though the fragrance of honey, and of these special Hungarian wines, partake of the same nature. It should be remembered that these wines are not made in the usual way, but are from grapes which have been allowed to reach a full ripeness, and then the juice is allowed to flow, we might almost say, *distil*, in its full richness into the vats, and from this comes Tokay and the other fine wines of the same kind. But all this labour, and special care, while it achieves an outstanding wine, achieves only what we have always had in properly, and finely, made and well-kept sack-mead. Old White Mount Hymetus, one of the finer Greek wines, has somewhat of these qualities, but it lies closer to the drier sack-meads, than the richer to which Tokay is near allied. It must, however, be remembered that as honey varies with district and race of bee, as well as from year to year, all sacks will not be alike. Consequently it would be a mistake to stress too far the similarity of some of them to such as Tokay. One old writer, for instance, whom Tickner Edwardes notes, made a sack-mead, indistinguishable from Canary Sack.[263]

It will be readily understood that such a drink as sack-mead meets all requirements ranging from the dry sweet wines, such as Sherry, to the dessert.

Metheglin. Metheglin, being made from substantially the

same *must* as mead, except for the addition of certain gruit (herbal) mixtures, the recipes of which are usually closely preserved secrets, has much the same qualities as mead, with a heightening of the flavours by the addition of the herbs. A liquor of mere table wine strength, and complete dryness, does not lend itself to spicing and so a plain metheglin is not to be recommended for general use.

Sack-metheglin. Sack-metheglin is to metheglin what sack is to mead, being, therefore, similar to sack-mead except for the spicing which makes the taste stronger, and submerges (but not without compensating qualities in return) some of the finer and more subtle flavours of the mead. It lies closer to the range of Vermouth wines in the principles involved in its making, and, although of a different flavour and bouquet, it is excellent for the same purposes.

Bochet is a burnt sack-mead, and has undergone in its making a parallel process to that which is common in preparing certain southern European wines, where heat is applied to reduce the water content either by partially drying the grapes (as in the case of Sherry) or actually boiling the juice as is sometimes the practice in Italy, as it was in Roman times. Bochet has a bouquet all its own and forms a dessert wine, as well as a tonic for invalids.

Cyser or Ciser, which is the genuine ancient " cider " or " strong-drink " is made not merely from apple juice, like modern cider, but also from honey. Consequently this is a wine of the strength of sack-mead, and in flavour and bouquet closer to the Sherries than any other of the mead liquors. It has quite a fine fragrance and is well qualified to fulfil all the uses of that wine as an appetiser.

Pyment being a mixture of a red wine and honey with the addition of spicings or *gruit* is in fact a red dessert wine of high flavour. The Roman *Mulsum* is of the same type, although, owing to the addition of water, it could not have had the same body and would normally only remain sweet when new, unless a great amount of honey were used in its making. There is little doubt that often enough the Romans must have resorted to making mulsum to correct the tartness of some of their wines, or else to soften the harshness of ill-tasting wines, which would be wonderfully improved by the use of honey. Perhaps Virgil was thinking principally of this latter use of honey in mulsum when he wrote in the *Georgics* (Book IV, 101–102)—" from this at the certain season of the year you will press sweet honey ; and yet not so sweet as crystal-clear, and able to subdue the harsh flavour of wine."

Hippocras is a variant of pyment, usually made with sugar rather than with honey. Where such a hippocras receives a spirituous fortification it is for all practical purposes in much the same category as such proprietary wines as Byrrh and Dubonnet.

Melomel is a wine of much the same type as pyment, except that fruit juices other than those of the grape enter into its making. It can range from the dry to the dessert type.

Bracket is, like cyser, pyment, mulsum and melomel, a hybrid liquor, in that, in this case, it is a compound of mead and ale.

Raspberry Sack-mead. This is like the preceding, a combination between a mead and fruit juices, in this case that of raspberries. It is a variant associated with Poland and other Eastern European countries. In Poland some of this raspberry sack has been known to obtain a considerable reputation, and to approach a liqueur in quality.

Such then are the chief varieties of the mead liquors, the whole range of which, completed with a mead brandy and a honey liqueur, fully furnish the wine services for all and every occasion, no matter how exacting may be the requirements.

CHAPTER XV

WASSAIL !

WITH the English drinking vessel, be it wood or silver, in our hands, and with the crystal sparkling old mead in the mazer, there still remains one thing yet to mention to round off the whole culture of English drinking, and that is the toast.

It is a curious thing that a nation which has such a tradition as that of mead, and such beautiful national vessels as the mazers, should not only have neglected any regard for these, but should also have almost lost in everyday custom the normal words of politeness which ought and must accompany the quaffing of a friendly cup in any civilized society. Hence it is that people so often hesitate and appear diffident before giving the toast on receiving the informal glass, for they seem as though they know not what to say : and it usually ends up with some shoddy, cheap, and vulgar " Cheers ! " " Cheerio ! " " Here's how ! " " What ho ! " " Chin-chin ! " or something that must come from the kennels or the stews called " Here's mud in your eyes ! " whatever it may mean.

But among other peoples there is no such difficulty—the German raises his glass to *Prost*, the Scandinavian to *Skol*, the Frenchman to *À bonne Santé*, the Celt to *Slaintè* and the Italian to *Salute*. Only the Englishman is apparently so denationalized, that he fears to use a plain English " Your health " and resorts to facetiousness, a fault in him, when not at ease, of which the whole world is aware excepting himself.

Yet, in the England of a former age there was no such difficulty. For, in fact, the English heritage of toasting is quite as rich as that of its liquor or its goblets, all of which need not take second place to those of any other land.

This then is my excuse for finishing this short account
of mead with, not only a brief description of the goblets
from which it was drunk, but with a slight mention of the
traditional toast, of which we have some record, which
accompanied the act of drinking.

We have already seen something, in passing, of the great
dignity of the toast among our Anglo-Saxon and Norse
ancestors in pagan times, and how it was even a part of the
ceremonial of the religious festival, both before and after the
establishment of Christianity :

" And first Odin's goblet was emptied for victory and power to
his kind ; thereafter, Njord's and Freya's goblets for peace and a
good season. Then it was the custom of many to empty the Brage
beaker ; and then the guests emptied a goblet to the memory of
departed friends, called the remembrance goblet."

. . . .

" Let us drink this cup in the name of the holy Archangel Michael,
begging and praying him to introduce our souls into the peace of
eternal exaltation."

But it is in *Beowulf* and *Geoffrey of Monmouth* that we come
to the more intimate toasting between the host and his
guests.

In those days, although there were small bowls or mazers,
it was more usual at the feast to have the great mazer, which
has survived as a grace-cup in the ceremonies of such old
corporations as the City Companies. This was, in a secular
sense, a communion bowl. The hostess approached the chief
guest or guests with it and offered them to drink from it,
wishing them health, and so they pledged each other.

" . . . went Wealtheow forth,

. . . .

That she to Beowulf | braceleted Queen,
Noble-maid | the mead-bowl bore."

. . . .

" . . . the damsel stepped forth of her chamber bearing a golden
cup filled with wine [*sic* mead], and coming next the King, bended
her knee and spake, saying : ' Laverd King, wacht heil ! ' . . .
Whereupon Vortigern made answer : ' Drinc heil ! ' . . . and from

that day unto this hath the custom held in Britain that he who
drinketh at a feast saith unto another, ' Wacht heil ! ' and he that
receiveth the drink after him maketh answer, ' Drinc heil ! ' "

Here we have the actual words used upon drinking a health
in England.   They are the old English *waes hael,* which is
literally " be whole ", meaning " be of good health ", or
" your health ".   Therefore, the health given by the beautiful
Princess Rowena to the Welsh King Vortigern was :

> " *Waes hael hlaford Cyning !* "
> (Be of Health, Lord King !)

That this health, and its formal answer " Drink, hail "
(presumably meaning in reply, " I drink your health ") lived
long in England after the time of Hengist is illustrated by the
last stanza of the earliest existing carol known, which was
probably one in use among the wandering minstrels of
Norman times :

> " Lords, by Christmas and the host
> of this mansion, hear my toast—
> Drink it well—
> Each must drain his cup of wine,
> And I the first will toss off mine :
> Thus I advise,
> Here then I bid you all *Wassail,*
> Cursed be he who will not say *Drink hail.*" [264]

Caxton's *Chronicle* in its account of the death of King John,
tells us that he was given a cup of good ale by a kneeling
monk, to the accompaniment of the traditional " Your health "
(*Wassail*) :

" Syr, *wassayll* for ever the dayes so all lyfe dranke ye of so good
a cuppe." [265]
(Sir, *Your health* ! you never drank of such a cup in all your life !)

At Christmas, which was naturally a time of great festivity
the master of the house gathered his family around the bowl
of wine, or mead or spiced ale, and passed it round to the
words " *Waes hael !* "

From this custom of drinking " Waes hael ! " (*Your*

health) it became the custom to talk of the bowl out of which the draught was taken as the *wassail* bowl, especially so when reference was made to the bowl at Christmas time and New Year, on which occasions a greater number of healths were pledged than at any other.

This led in time to the contents of the bowl, which was generally brewed for Christmas, also being called " Wassail ". Such " Wassail " compositions by reason of the cold damp part of the year in which they were used were sweet and highly spiced hot " punches " of sorts, and as the liquor was drunk in great quantities by all classes, the bases of the draught varied according to the circumstances of those who drank, we may presume that besides wines, ciders, beers and ales, meads were also used in making the *wassail* bowl ? In Poland to this day, mead is still sold and drunk hot in the taverns in cold weather.

Washington Irving [266] tells us something of the composition of this Christmas liquor in the early nineteenth century :

" The Wassail Bowl was sometimes composed of ale instead of wine ; with nutmeg, sugar, toast, ginger, and roasted crabs ; in this way the nut-brown beverage is still prepared in some old families and round the hearths of substantial farmers at Christmas. It is also called Lambs' Wool and is celebrated by Herrick in his *Twelfth Night* :

> ' Next crowne the bowle full
> With gentle Lambs' Wool,
> And sugar, nutmeg and ginger,
> With store of ale too ;
> And thus ye must doe
> To make the Wassaile a swinger.' "

It is obviously to this *wassail* bowl that Shakespeare alludes :

> " When all aloud the wind doth blow,
>   And coughing drowns the parson's saw,
> And birds sit brooding in the snow,
>   And Marian's nose looks red and raw,
> When roasted crabs hiss in the bowl,
> Then nightly sings the staring owl,
>   To-whit ! "

L

The custom of the *wassail* bowl is maintained by Jesus College where a large silver-gilt bowl (given to the college by Sir Watkin W. Wynne in 1732) is used.

Not only did the words of the pledge become used, as they became archaic, for the bowl and its contents at Christmas time, but the words became the name for the custom of " wassailing ". This custom was that of going around to neighbours' houses to sing, and to present to the householders a *wassail* bowl in return for which a gift was given. The following (from Gloucestershire) is an example of one of these typical *wassail* songs, of interest also because it tells us that the bowl from which the *wassail* was drunk was a wooden mazer of maple wood :

> " Wassail ! Wassail ! over the town,
> Our toast it is white, our ale it is brown :
> Our bowl it is made of the maplin tree,
> We be good fellows all ; I drink to thee." [267]

It would seem that the actual Anglo-Saxon words for " Your health ! " were in usage at Christmas as late as the reign of Henry VII, the first Tudor King of England, although their archaic form had probably led to their disappearance at other times of the year. For we read that in the ordinances for the regulation of the court, on Twelfth Night, the steward of the household was commanded to enter with the piping *wassail* bowl and to say three times " Waes Hael ! "

The *wassail* bowl was, apparently, and with it no doubt the customary pledge, in fashion as late as the time of Charles I.

The use of the word *wassail* was also preserved late in the custom of *wassailing* fruit trees on Twelfth Night in the West Country. The drinking of healths to trees, and the doing of it three times, as was the custom, is so like the Scandinavian custom of pledging the three gods that it suggests that the custom must have come down from pagan Anglo-Saxon or Scandinavian sources.

Apparently the farmer and his servants carried a *wassail* of steaming cider and roasted crab-apples to the orchard and

formed a ring round their best tree and *wassailed* it three
times, to the following :

> " Here's to thee, old apple-tree,
> Whence thou may'st bud, and may'st blow !
> And whence thou may'st bear apples enow !
> Hats full ! caps full !
> Bushel—bushel—sacks full !
> And my pockets full too ! Huzza ! " [268]

There were, of course, at all ages other forms of toast, as
may be expected, than *Waes hael!*

The " *Drink hael* " (I drink your health), which was the
appropriate reply to " *Waes hael!* " tended to become a
pledge itself at one period, in the simple command " Drink ! "
or " Drink you ! " While at all times there have been incidental pledges for the occasion. " I pledge you " was for a
long time a typical English expression of toasting with many
traditions associated with it. In the following quaint quotation, several centuries old, of a Frenchman's account of the
English drinking habits, as he happened to experience some
of them, we find him mentioning " I pledge you " and " Drink
you ", for I presume that is what his " Drind iou " means :

" The English, one with another, are joyous, and are very fond
of music ; for there is not ever so small a church in which music
is not sung : and they are great drinkers ; for if an Englishman
wishes to treat you, he will say to you in his language, *vil dring a
quarta rim oim gas-quim, oim hespaignol, oim malvoysi ?* which means,
*veulez tu venir boire une quarte de vin du gascoigne, une autre d'espaigne,
et une autre de malvoise ?* In drinking and in eating, they will say
to you more than a hundred times, *drind iou* ; and you will reply
to them in their language, *iplaigiu.* If you thank them, you will
say to them in their language, *god tanque artelay.* Being drunk,
they will swear to you by blood and death that you shall drink all
that you hold in your cup, and you will say thus, *bigod sol drind
iou agoud oiu.* Now, remember (if you please) that in this country
they generally use vessels of silver when they drink wine ; and they
will say to you usually at table, *goud chere.* " [269]

Perhaps the unpleasant " Cheerio ! " is a corruption of the
more dignified " Good cheer ! "

Despite these other forms of toasting, the fact remains, that
as the words " *Waes hael!* " became so old-fashioned that

eventually they were not understood at all, their translation,
" Your health " passed into common use.   So that the pledge
which has the longest tradition, and is with us still, is " *wassail!* " or " Your health ", and this may be rightly acclaimed
the English toast.

The reader then I pledge :

" Wassail ! "

in

Mazers of Mead.

" . . . and from that day unto this hath the custom held in Britain
that he who drinketh at a feast saith unto another, ' Wacht heil ! '
and he that receiveth the drink after him maketh answer ' Drink
heil ! ' "

BREWING
MEAD

by Charlie Papazian
A Founding Member of
Friends of Mead

Easy, Step-by-Step
Instructions
for Brewing It At Home

PREFACE

THE FRIENDS OF MEAD

A FRIEND of mead is a friend, indeed. Mead is the beverage for all seasons, for all continents, for all cultures. This fermented nectar of honey and water is especially celebrated with this new edition of *Brewing Mead*. We especially acknowledge Lt. Colonel Robert Gayre, of Gayre & Nigg, for granting us permission to reprint his original work, *Wassail! In Mazers of Mead.*

We recognize Lt. Colonel Gayre as the world's foremost authority on the history of mead. His research and writings have elevated mead's stature to one of deserved significance as man's first fermented beverage—a beverage revered in many diverse cultures and prized as mankind's initial experience with the joys of fermented beverage.

We wish to thank Lt. Colonel Gayre for contributing his time and efforts on behalf of the mead fancier. We also wish to acknowledge and thank the following people as Charter members of The Friends of Mead for their contribution in making this publication possible: Daniel Bradford, John and Lois Canaday, Alan Dikty, Diane and Dick Dunn, Gretchen Graff, Jeffrey and Peggy Markel, Kathy McClurg, Grosvenor and Rosemarie Merle-Smith, Charlie Papazian, Jeannie Roberts, Kaye Tompkins, and Brent Warren.

Wassail!

Brewers Publications

CHAPTER XVI

INTRODUCTION TO BREWING MEAD

MEAD is a fermented beverage unto itself. It is neither a beer nor a wine. This fact must be remembered throughout its formulation and brewing process and finally, kept in mind when sampling the final product. For most, mead brewing is a wonderfully new and rewarding experience—a spirituous indulgence into the traditions we have inherited from thousands of years of brewing.

Brewing mead and its variations is a simple process requiring patience. Homebrewers and home wine makers will find they are already familiar with the basic process of formulation and fermentation for brewing mead, but most will newly discover the uniquely enjoyable results of this traditionally made drink.

No one should ever use the excuse that mead takes too long to make. Time passes. And what better way is there to pass time than knowing that one's mead is slowly aging, mellowing, and maturing as he or she is?

CHAPTER XVII

TYPES OF MEAD AND THEIR VARIATIONS

L T. Colonel Gayre tells us that there are five basic categories of mead. Here is a summary of the classic types.

Traditional Mead—This is the basic mead brewed from honey and water in the proportions of approximately two and a half pounds per one U.S. gallon (three pounds per one Imperial gallon).

Sack Mead—This sauternelike beverage is brewed similarly to traditional mead, except for the addition of 20 to 25 percent more honey. Traditionally, sack mead should not smell like honey when it is opened; therefore, too much honey should not be used.

Metheglin—Metheglin is a special mead made with the addition of *gruit*. Gruit is a combination of herbs that were supplied to mead makers and brewers in the Middle Ages by monastic monks. Later, with the introduction of hops, a fierce competition arose between the Roman Catholic Church and the growers of the newly introduced hops. Eventually the hop growers won, mostly because hops were an inexpensive substitute for the herbs, thus inspiring the popularity of hops.

Sack Metheglin—Like sack mead, this is a metheglin made with more honey. Traditionally it was a drink similar to vermouth, which was probably derived from sack metheglin.

Fruit Juices and Mead—There are four basic types of meads produced from mixing honey with fruit juices and then fermenting the mixture. They are as follows:

Clarre or Pyment—Originating from Bordeaux, this ferment is a mixture of grape juice and honey. Clarre was a popular drink in the Middle Ages, and Lt. Colonel Gayre believes that this beverage eventually gave rise to claret.

Cyser—A ferment of apple cider (juice) and honey produces a beverage called *cyser*, from which the name cider is derived. In Biblical times, this was the "strong drink" so often referred to, as it is very alcoholic and almost like a sherry wine in flavor.

Mulsum or Melomel—A ferment of honey, water, and fruit juice(s) other than apples or grapes, this drink was popular in Roman times.

Morat—Morat is a ferment made from honey, water, and mulberries.

There is one additional beverage made from the fermentation of honey: *Mead Brandy*. Although illegal to distill on a homebrewing level, mead brandy is distilled from mead. It is quite unique in that it is ready to drink as it comes from the still because the mead from which it is made does not contain impurities that have to be "aged," as is the case with brandy and whiskey. Mead brandy liqueurs can be made by the addition of honey to sweeten the spirit. It is thought that the whiskey and honey liquor called *Drambuie* is probably derived from such a mead brandy liqueur.

CHAPTER XVIII

THE PROCESS

MAKING mead is a process whereby honey and water are formulated and then fermented by yeasts. *Yeasts* are microorganisms either naturally in the honey or introduced by the mead maker. The life process of yeast cells transforms sugars (from the honey or fruit) into carbon dioxide, alcohol, and the unique flavors of mead.

Once the yeasts consume all of the sugars in the formulation, they settle to the bottom of the fermentation vessel. Upon complete fermentation and clearing, the mead is bottled and then consumed or aged for the flavor changes that time causes.

A home mead maker needs some basic equipment, much of which he may already have at hand.

Equipment

Equipment needed for brewing in five-gallon batches:
1 four-gallon enameled or stainless steel pot (optional)
2 five-gallon glass carboys (for fermentation)
1 fermentation lock with rubber cork to fit carboy
7 feet clear plastic 5/16-inch inside diameter (siphoning) hose
3 feet clear plastic 5/16-inch inside diameter (blow-out) hose
Corker or bottlecapper
Corks or bottlecaps
Bottles
Wine hydrometer
Thermometer
Funnel (for funneling into carboy fermenters)

Other useful items used during the mead-making process are:

Acid-testing kit
Sodium or potassium metabisulphite
Acid blend
Yeast nutrients
All of the above equipment and accessory ingredients are available at home wine- and beer-making supply shops throughout the country.

Specific Gravity and Your Hydrometer

The Specific Gravity is an indirect measure of the sugar content of the mead that is to be fermented. The measurement can easily be accomplished by immersing a wine or beer hydrometer into a sample of the honey and water mixture. The level at which the hydrometer floats gives a reading indicating the sugar content of the solution being measured.

A Note on Honey

Honey is derived from the nectar of flowers and is processed and ripened with the aid of enzymes secreted by the honeybee. Because the source of nectar can vary, so does the quality and taste of the honey. There are thousands of different kinds of honey, but mostly they are comprised of glucose and fructose sugars with trace amounts of sucrose and maltose. The water content of honey is usually less than 15 percent; above this then, the honey is susceptible to fermentation in the hive. The color and flavor is the most significant and recognizable difference to the mead maker.

Lighter honeys such as clover and alfalfa are often considered to be the best for mead making because of their minimal contribution of strong flavors. This view of "best" may be debatable as traditional mead was most likely made with whatever honey was available, usually wild and mixed blossoms.

Modern mead making and present-day palates may best begin with lighter honeys and embark upon experimentation after experience has been gained. It must be noted that modern-day honey most often lacks desired mead-fermenting yeast and yeast nutrients. For a consistent, dependable, controllable fermentation quality, cultured wine yeasts and yeast nutrients must be added. When making simple mead, it is often desirable to add a small quantity of "acid blend" (a combination of 25 percent citric, 30 percent malic, and 45 percent tartaric acids) to the ferment. Honey alone lacks acidity, a characteristic that many people consider favorable in mead. If a traditional mead were desired, then any addition of acidity would not be called for.

A Note on Fermentation

The science of fermentation is both simple and complex. It is a process through which tiny, one-celled yeasts metabolize sugars into various byproducts that include, in our special mead-making case, carbon dioxide, alcohol, and mead flavors. A few points especially helpful for the mead maker are highlighted here:

• Yeasts require nutrients (absent in modern-day honey) in order to sustain healthy fermentation. Therefore, the addition of yeast nutrients ensures proper fermentation for the home mead maker.

• An adequate supply of yeast must be added, or *pitched*, to the mixture of honey and water (and herbs or fruit juices) to produce healthy, quick, complete fermentation. One should always follow the directions that are supplied with the cultured wine or Champagne yeast he uses. When in doubt, use more. This is especially critical when using liquid cultures.

• Yeast must have an adequate supply of oxygen during the initial twelve-to-eighteen-hour phase of "fermentation." After this period, care must be taken **not** to introduce oxygen to the fermentation.

Adequate supplies of oxygen can easily be supplied to the yeast by vigorously pouring or shaking the unfermented honey and water. Cold tap water also contains ample amounts of oxygen in solution. Without proper initial aeration, sluggish and prolonged fermentations occur, although it is often typical of meads to ferment very slowly for months. In any case, don't worry; be patient.

• Raw or unpasteurized honey is likely to contain wild yeast and bacteria. When diluted with water, these natural microorganisms may cause spontaneous and undesirable fermentations yielding unpalatable flavors and poor stability. The procedures in this book recommend pasteurizing the honey by boiling or by the addition of sodium metabisulphite in small quantities as is commonly done in the practice of wine making. Either method kills or inhibits the undesirable yeasts and bacteria and enhances the environment for the healthy fermentation of cultured yeast.

Traditionally, such precautions and procedures were unheard of. Honey and water spontaneously fermented, usually producing a fairly consistent product. But we must remember that beekeeping practices are quite different today. As a consequence, natural yeast is not available. Also, today, we are likely to buy our honey, not knowing its origins. And if we know them, we are unable to assure its consistency and quality.

If your inclination for experimentation and tradition gets the better of you, of course, as a home mead maker, you are free to experiment. A word of suggestion might be to experiment in small, one-gallon batches.

CHAPTER XIX

RECIPES AND MEASURES

RECIPES and procedures are necessary for modern mead makers, although our forebears undoubtedly used "a pinch of this, a slug of that, and a handful of the other." These recipes and procedures have all been updated and written keeping in mind the ingredients and equipment available to modern fermenters, as well as our advanced understanding today of the technology of brewing.

Notes: Temperatures are expressed in degrees Fahrenheit with degrees Celsius in parentheses. For U.S. recipes, weights are in pounds and ounces. British weights are given in both pounds, ounces, and the metric system and are in brackets.

Recipes

"Wassail" Mead

Ingredients for:	5 U.S. gal.	5 Imperial gal.
Light clover honey	12.5 lbs. [5.7 kg]	15 lbs. [6.8 kg]
Acid blend	4 tsp.	5 tsp.
Yeast nutrient	5 tsp.	6 tsp.
Water to make	5 U.S. gal.	5 Imp. gal.
Adequate wine yeast		

1/3 tsp. sodium or potassium metabisulphite for procedure number 2

Original Specific Gravity 1.110

Procedure Number 1:

Add honey, acid blend, and yeast nutrient to two gallons of water and boil for one half hour in a large pot to pasteurize honey. Add 1 1/2 gallons of cold water to a sanitized glass fermenter. Using a funnel, pour the hot honey water into the fermenter and cold water. Top up with cold water to make five gallons. Add yeast when temperature is 70 to 75 degrees F (21 to 24 degrees C).

Procedure Number 2:

Add honey, acid blend, and yeast nutrient to one gallon of hot tap water to blend and dissolve honey. Add to sanitized fermenter with enough cold water to make five gallons. Add sodium metabisulphite and let stand for at least twenty-four hours with the top of the fermenter allowed to release sulfur dioxide gas from the fermenter.

(NOTE: It has been discovered that a very small number of people who suffer from asthma may have adverse reactions to sulfur dioxide in wines and many other foods. If in doubt, consult your physician.)

Add yeast after this twenty-four-hour disinfecting period.

Because of mead's often slow fermentation, it is advisable from a sanitation standpoint to ferment mead in a closed fermenter. A *closed fermenter* is one that is sealed away from ambient air yet allows for overflow foaming and carbon dioxide gas to escape. This method of closed fermentation can most easily be achieved by fermenting in glass carboys. (In the U.S., carboys are usually 5- or 6 1/2-gallon glass containers with a narrow neck and opening.)

When the honey, water, and yeast mixture is added to the carboy, fermentation will soon begin. When this happens, there is vigorous foaming during the initial stages. A drilled rubber cork with a three-foot plastic tube leading out into a catch bucket allows foam to be expelled. When vigorous fermentation has subsided, then the hose may be removed and a standard fermentation lock can be affixed, allowing gas to escape during the ensuing period of fermentation.

Allow fermentation to proceed at 65 to 75 degrees F (18 to 24 degrees C) in an area away from direct sunlight or bright, direct, artificial light. Initial fermentation may take from three weeks to many months, depending on the type of honey, yeast, temperature, etc. When initial fermentation is complete, the yeast settles to the bottom of the fermenter and the mead becomes fairly clear.

After the mead is clear, siphon it off, leaving the sediment behind, into another clean and sanitized fermenter. Care should be taken not to splash the mead as it enters the new fermenter. Attach the fermentation lock to the second fermenter.

During its time in the secondary fermenter, the mead may undergo a "secondary fermentation."

At any rate, leave the mead to sit for at least three weeks or until secondary fermentation is complete and the yeast once again settles to the bottom as a sediment.

When the mead is clear, it is ready to bottle.

Bottling Procedures

All equipment and bottles must be cleaned and sanitized before use. Immersing equipment and bottles in a solution of one ounce of household bleach in five gallons of cold water is a very effective sanitizer. Rinse bottles and equipment thoroughly with hot tap water.

When transferring the mead by siphon, take care not to aerate it, as oxidation dramatically changes the flavor of mead to its detriment. Quietly siphon the mead into the bottles it will be served from.

Beer and Champagne bottles may be filled and capped with standard bottle caps using a bottlecapper.

Wine bottles may also be used and sealed with corks. These are best laid on their side while in storage in order to prevent the cork from drying out. If sidewise storage is not possible or practical, simply dip the cork end of the bottle in melted parafin. This prevents the cork from drying out and ruining the seal.

Sparkling Mead

If sparkling mead is desired, standard Champagne bottling procedures may be followed. Generally, sparkling mead would have to be of lesser strength in order for the yeast to survive a second fermentation in the bottle; it should generally not have original specific gravity over 1.090.

In the case of mead allowed to become crystal clear in the carboy over a long period of time, it is necessary to not only add additional priming sugar to the bottle but also a fresh, active yeast source.

Sparkling mead is achieved simply by adding honey or sugar at the rate of 3/4 to one *cup* (caution: do not misinterpret as pounds!) for every five gallons. Simply boil and dissolve the "priming" sugar in eight ounces of water, and add it to the bulk mead that has been racked into another fermenter leaving behind any sediment. Stir to disperse sugar. Fresh yeast may be added at this time also.

Over a period of time, a small amount of fermentation will occur in the bottle and throw a sediment of yeast. The mead can be decanted off the sediment when served or a more elaborate process of removing the sediment can be done.

As with Champagne, after the mead has been primed and capped with bottle caps, the bottles are stored upside down. The yeast sediment then accumulates in the neck of the bottle. From time to time, the bottles should be given a quick turn to dislodge yeast adhering to the sides of the bottle. After the mead has cleared and it is apparent that the mead has completed sedimentation, the necks of the bottles are immersed in an ice and salt brine, thus freezing the sediment at the neck. The bottles are carefully righted, uncapped, and the frozen yeast "plug" is gently forced out of the bottle by the pressure generated during the carbonating process. The bottles may then be resealed with caps or corks.

Sack Mead

Ingredients for:	5 U.S. gal.	5 Imperial gal.
Light clover honey	15 lbs. [6.8 kg]	18 lbs. [8.2 kg]
Acid blend	4 tsp.	5 tsp.
Yeast nutrient	6 tsp.	7 tsp.
Water to make	5 U.S. gallons	5 Imperial gal.

Adequate wine yeast

1/3 tsp. sodium or potassium metabisulphite for procedure number 2

Approximate Original Specific Gravity 1.120 to 1.130

Follow procedures outlined for Wassail Mead.

Metheglin

Ingredients for:	5 U.S. gal.	5 Imperial gal.
Light clover honey	12.5 lbs. [5.7 kg]	15 lbs. [6.8 kg]
Acid blend	4 tsp.	5 tsp.
Yeast nutrient	5 tsp.	6 tsp.
Water to make	5 U.S. gal.	5 Imperial gal.

Adequate wine yeast. Other quality types of wine or Champagne yeast may be used.

1/3 tsp. sodium metabisulphite for procedure number 2

Gruit

1 oz. of fresh hops

OR 1 to 2 oz. of freshly grated ginger

OR 2 to 4 oz. lemongrass

OR 1 to 2 oz. crushed cinnamon bark

OR crushed fennel, anise, caraway, clove seeds

OR crushed hot chile pepper (with or without seeds)

OR a combination of these and any other spice, herb, bark, and seeds fit for human consumption

Approximate Original Specific Gravity 1.110

Follow the procedures for making Wassail Mead, except at bottling time or after vigorous fermentation has subsided, make a strong tea with the gruit ingredients you have chosen to use and add them at bottling time.

Sack Metheglin

Combine Sack Mead recipe with formulation of gruits from Metheglin recipe.

Pyment or Clarre

Ingredients for:	5 U.S. gal.	5 Imperial gal.
Light clover honey	7 lbs. [3.2 kg]	8.5 lbs. [3.9 kg.]
Grape juice	2 1/2 gal.	2 1/2 gal.
Water to make	5 U.S. gal.	5 Imperial gal.
Yeast nutrient	5 tsp.	6 tsp.

Adequate wine yeast

1/3 tsp. sodium metabisulphite

An adequate amount of acid blend to bring acid level to .4 to .5 percent level. Acid test kits are inexpensive and may be bought at any home wine making supply shop. Instructions are clear and simple to understand.

Approximate Original Specific Gravity 1.100 to 1.120

Procedure number two, using sodium metabisulphite, should be followed. (**CAUTION:** Do not add grape skins to closed glass fermenter as they will plug the escape vent and cause explosion. See procedures for Mulsum and Melomel if fermentation with skins is desired.)

It is not desirable to boil grapes or any other fruit juice as the fruit pectin will "set" and the mead may not clarify as a result.

Ferment and bottle as you would a mead.

Cyser

Ingredients for:	5 U.S. gal.	5 Imperial gal.
Light clover honey	7 lbs. [3.2 kg]	8.5 lbs [3.9 kg]
Apple juice (approx.)	4 3/4 gallons	4 3/4 gallons
Yeast nutrient	5 tsp.	6 tsp.

Adequate wine yeast

1/3 tsp. sodium or potassium metabisulphite.

An adequate amount of acid blend to bring acid level to .4 to .5 percent level. Acid test kits are inexpensive and may be bought at any home wine making supply shop. Instructions are clear and simple to understand.

Approximate Original Specific Gravity 1.100 to 1.115

Procedure number two using metabisulphite should be followed. It is not desirable to boil grape or any other fruit juice because the fruit pectin will "set" and the mead may not clarify as a result.

Ferment and bottle as you would a mead.

Mulsum or Melomel

Ingredients for: 5 U.S. gal.   5 Imperial gal.

Light clover honey	9 lbs. [4.1 kg]	11 lbs. [5 kg]
Crushed fruit	10-15 lbs.	12-18 lbs.
	[4.5-6.8 kg]	[5.5-8.2 kg.]

Raspberries, blueberries, blackberries, marionberries, loganberries, mangoes, currants, peaches, plums, cherries, and many others may be considered.

Yeast nutrient	5 tsp.	6 tsp.
Water to make	5 U.S. gal.	5 Imperial gal.

Adequate wine yeast
1/3 tsp. sodium metabisulphite.
An adequate amount of acid blend to bring acid level to .4 to .5 percent level. Acid test kits are inexpensive and may be bought at any home wine making supply shop. Instructions are clear and simple to understand.

Approximate Original Specific Gravity 1.100 to 1.120

Procedure number two, using sodium metabisulphite, should be followed. It is not desirable to boil any fruit juice because the fruit pectin will "set" and the mead may not clarify as a result.

However, procedure number two may be used if the honey is boiled first and the crushed fruit added and allowed to steep for thirty minutes at 160 degrees F.

Fermentation procedures vary with mulsum or melomel because the crushed fruit is carried over to the fermentation; thus an open-type fermenter must be used during the first five to ten days of fermentation. An *open fermenter* is a clean fermentation bucket or pail snugly fit with aluminum foil or a sheet of plastic which allows gases to escape.

After five to ten days of fermentation, the fruit is strained out with a sterilized strainer (boil in water for twenty minutes). The remaining ferment is then siphoned off into a closed glass fermenter. Some fruit will unavoidably be carried into the second fermenter. After two weeks, or when vigorous fermentation has subsided, siphon ferment into a third fermenter leaving virtually all of the fruit sediment and some yeast sediment behind.

Complete the fermentation and bottle from this point as you would a mead.

Mead Brandy

Although illegal to make at home, it is interesting to note that alcohol boils at 173 degrees F and has the ability to condense on cool surfaces. It is easily collected as it drips from the condenser. Temperatures above 173 degrees F result in some of the mead liquor also being evaporated and condensed.

CHAPTER XX

CONCLUSION

MEAD can be brewed by anyone. It has so many variations, it is sure to keep mead makers and adventurers busy for a lifetime. Mead provides a wonderful choice in brewing and drinking. It is an opportunity for choice that has been passed on through the ages, and as a mead maker, you can become a part of keeping a very special tradition alive and well.

Perhaps in the coming years we shall see quality mead being made available to many more individuals. It is not too far fetched to anticipate commercial meaderies making quality mead we all can be proud to call real mead. Through our own efforts as mead makers and the inspiration we give in every bottle we share with friends, we will see a mead renaissance.

To you, the mead maker, we raise a glass in salute, "Wassail! In mazers of mead."

REFERENCES AND NOTES

1. " An Ale " meant a parish festival. The word *bridal* is really *bride-ale*—the wedding feast.
2. Several interesting notices of Church, Easter and Whitsun Ales will be found in A. R. Wright, *British Calendar Customs*, Vol. I, London, 1936.
3. *Rig-Veda*, I, 154, 4–6, translated by A. Macdonell.
4. *Rig-Veda*, VIII, 48.
5. We read in a seventeenth-century work of the Welsh metheglin —" They have likewise metheglin—compounded of milk and honey and [it] is very wholesome." *History of the Principality of Wales :* Printed by Nath. Church, London, 1695.
6. Virgil, *Aeneid*, XII, 383–440.
7. Virgil, *Georgics*, IV, 415.
8. J. Grimm, in his *Teutonic Mythology*, identifies *amrita, nectar* and *ambrosia* with the magic mead.
9. " *Ion* " *and the Four Dialogues of Plato ;* from P. B. Shelley's translation of *The Banquet*, Everyman Library, 1913, p. 51.
10. Porphyry, *De Abstin.*, II, 20.
11. Plutarch, *Banquet*, 106.
12. *Odyssey*, X, 519.
13. Alciphron, translated by F. A. Wright, Broadway Translations, London, p. 189.
14. Hilda M. Ransome, *The Sacred Bee*, London, 1937, p. 285. The Hindu novice for the priesthood had to abstain from meat, women, perfumes, and honey. Beck & Smedley, *Honey and Your Health*, London, 1947, p. 117.
15. Leon Arnon, *Manuel du Confiseur-Liquoriste*, Paris, 1905, p. 4. The French consider both honey and the bee-sting to have a powerful aphrodisiac quality. Beck & Smedley, *op. cit.*, p. 117.
16. Beck & Smedley, *op. cit.*, p. 21. One fails to understand, in the light of the historical regard for the love-stimulating qualities of honey (*or* mead), their contention that " from the medical standpoint, there is no basis for the assumption that honey is an aphrodisiac." Surely this is a confusion of terms, as these qualities would seem to belong rather to mead than honey from the traditional point of view. But, in addition, as they admit, and, indeed, contend, that honey has great re-vitalizing qualities, surely this is tantamount to saying that honey is a natural or true aphrodisiac !
17. Virgil, *Georgics*, IV, 51–66.
18. Pan, like Priapus, was a fertility god, and the nymphs were lesser divinities concerned with marriage and procreation.

19. Calpurnius, II, 64.
20. Crinagoras, *Anthology*, VI, 232.
21. *The Satyricon of Petronius.* Beck & Smedley, *op. cit.*, p. 117, rightly remind us that—" Honey was an important ingredient of all ancient Satyriaca (ad coitum irritantia tentaginem facientia)."
22. Dr. van der Flier, *Bulletin de la Soc. d'Apiculture des Alpes-Maritimes*, April–May, 1930 : *The Bee World*, Vol. XI, p. 93.
23. Lucius Apuleus, *The Golden Asse*, The Abbey Classics Edition, X.
24. Theocritus, VII, 147–155, *The Harvest Home*, transl. by J. M. Edmonds, The Greek Bucolic Poets, London, 1912, pp. 99–100.
25. Hilda M. Ransome, *op. cit.*, p. 158, quoting Glock, *Die Symbolik der Bienen*, p. 230. No doubt this association of mead with the gifts of wisdom, tongues and poetry, included, within its scope, the knowledge of the past, since we find such an association in the account of Odin where he visited Saga, the patroness of History, and quaffed with her from a goblet of gold, a draught of mead.
26. Theocritus, *op. cit.*, 78–85.
27. Hilda M. Ransome, *op. cit.*, p. 134, very rightly takes the same view that it was the mysterious qualities .of mead which led to its being regarded as the drink of the gods.
28. This is a view also taken by O. Schrader, *Prehistoric Antiquities of the Aryans*, p. 321 ; and G. L. Gomme, *Ethnology in Folklore*, London, 1892, p. 127 n.
29. A. Hislop, *The Two Babylons*, 1929, p. 194.
30. Chilperic Edwards, *The World's Earliest Laws*, London, 1937, p. 85.
31. *Ut supra*, pp. 28–29.
32. In the text there is written " wine-seller " and " wine-shop ". But this must be a mistake in translation and should be liquor- or beer-seller, as wine was not drunk in Babylonia. Chilperic Edwards, *op. cit.*, p. 85.
33. Pliny, Book XIV, 22. Posidonius, *apud. Athenaeus*, 152, tells us of a drink made from wheat in western Spain and Britain. Presumably this is the same *beer* to which Pliny alludes.
34. Isaac Taylor, *The Origin of the Aryans*, London, 1892, p. 170.
35. And in 1483 the ale-brewers petitioned the Lord Mayor of London to forbid the putting into the liquor of any hops or other herbs. *Encyclopaedia Britannica*, 14th edition, Vol. III, p. 314.
36. *Strabo*, IV, 5, 5.
37. In Avestan, a very ancient eastern Aryan tongue nearly related to the Sanskrit, the word *madu* had come to mean only mead. Likewise, in Lithuanian, the oldest surviving western Aryan language the double meaning had also been lost, and *medus* means mead. But we find in Chinese that the word for honey is *me*, and it is clear that this word must have been

borrowed from the Aryan not only on account of its similarity but also because, as Hilda M. Ransome, *op. cit.*, p. 52, points out, honey has no place in ancient Chinese and Japanese mythology. Therefore the use by the Chinese of an Aryan word for honey which is identical with that used in some Aryan languages for mead, and for honey and mead in Sanskrit, lends valuable support to the view that mead originally must have meant honey.

38. *Rig-Veda*, VIII, 48, translated by A. Macdonell.

39. T. Petronius Arbiter, The *Satyricon*, Barnaby's translation, 1694.

40. *Tacitus*, Chap. XVIII.

41. For instance, lines 1029, 1915, 2867, *Widsith, Beowulf, Finnsburgh, Waldere, Deor*, done into Common English, etc., by Charles Scott Moncrieff, London, 1921.

42. *Ut supra*, lines 480–483.

43. *Ut supra*, lines 491–496. Sweet in his paraphrase of *Beowulf* has the butler or cupbearer (here translated by Scott Moncrieff as a " thegn ") bearing not only ale but mead to the drinkers. See H. Sweet, *First Steps in Anglo-Saxon*, Oxford, 1897, p. 97, where we have :

> " þa behèold sebyrele swīþe wel his
> note : ēode æfter benĉum, and
> medo sĉęncte and hlutor ealo."

This *hlutor ealo* was ale of a superior kind, and apparently a *clear* ale. Reference to it is to be found in a grant of Offa, Sharon Turner, *History of the Anglo-Saxons*, 1820, Vol. 3, p. 35, where it is mentioned with mild and Welsh ale. (" 2 tuns of hlutres aloth, a cumb full of lithes aloth, and a cumb full of Welisces aloth.")

44. *Widsith, Beowulf*, etc., *op. cit.*, lines 2020–2023.

45. *Ut supra*, line 69.

46. *Ut supra*, lines 484, 638, 838.

47. *Ut supra*, lines 67–74.

48. *Ut supra*, lines 776, 1053, 1067.

49. *Ut supra*, lines 775–777.

50. *Ut supra*, lines 612–628.

51. *Ut supra*, lines 1980–1983.

52. *Geoffrey of Monmouth, Histories of the Kings of Britain*, London, 1920, Book VI, Chap. XII, pp. 106–107.

53. At the time of the massacre of the British nobles by Hengist the Welsh bard Golyddan sings, describing the banquet : " Conceive the intoxication at the great banquet of mead." *Gol. Arym*, 2. W. Arch. 156, after Sharon Turner, *op. cit.*, Vol. I, p. 246. From this we may conclude, as is certainly more probable, that Geoffrey's cup of " wine " was really one of mead.

54. *Ut supra*, lines 2015–7.

55. *Ut supra*, lines 918–924.
56. C. K. Scott Moncrieff, *ut supra*, p. 120, footnote to line 1643.
57. *Heimskringla, the Norse King Sagas*, by Snorre Sturlason, translated by Samuel Laing, London, 1930, p. 47.
58. *Heimskringla, op. cit.*, p. 93.
59. It is possible, however, that we should accept the date of King Hakon (tenth century) to which the account refers rather than the date when the *Heimskringla* was written.
60. *Heimskringla, op. cit.*, p. 94.
61. *Heimskringla, op. cit.*, p. 330.
62. *Heimskringla, op. cit.*, p. 121.
63. *Heimskringla, op. cit.*, p. 242.
64. *Heimskringla, op. cit.*, p. 72. Tore was brother of Rollo, the conqueror of Normandy.
65. *Heimskringla, op. cit.*, p. 124.
66. *Heimskringla, op. cit.*, pp. 15–16.
67. *Widsith, Beowulf*, etc., *op. cit.*, p. 106, lines 37–42. *Heimskringla, op. cit.*, p. 415.
68. *Poetic Edda, Lokasenna*, V. 6, p. 154.
69. *Heimskringla, op. cit.*, p. 70.
70. F. W. Hackwood, *Inns, Ale and Drinking Customs of Old England*, 1910, p. 38.
71. Sharon Turner, *op. cit.*, p. 38.
72. Sharon Turner, *op. cit.*, p. 355.
73. Sharon Turner, *op. cit.*, p. 36.
74. *William of Malmesbury* speaks of a vineyard attached to his monastery, which was first planted at the beginning of the eleventh century by a Greek monk who settled there, and who spent all his time in cultivating it. William of Malmesbury praised the Gloucestershire vines and the wine coming from them, rating it as only a little inferior to the wine which was brought from France.
75. R. K. Gordon, *Anglo-Saxon Poetry*, London, 1942, pp. 92–93.
76. R. K. Gordon, *op. cit.*, p. 330.
77. Paul Super, *The Polish Tradition*, London, 1941, p. 120.
78. R. K. Gordon, *op. cit.*, p. 351.
79. *The Mabinogion*, translated by Lady Charlotte Guest, London, pp. 150–151.
80. *The Mabinogion, op. cit.*, p. 408.
81. *The Mabinogion, op. cit.*, p. 367.
82. *The Mabinogion, op. cit.*, p. 355.
83. H. MacLean, *Ultonian Hero-Ballads*, Glasgow, 1892, p. 135.
84. Sharon Turner, *op. cit.*, Vol. I, p. 295.
85. It may be remarked, in passing, that Anglesey long maintained its reputation for mead. It was regarded, by Queen Elizabeth, as providing the best mead, and she drew annually large quantities of it from her ancestral Tudor home at Penmynydd. The name of an Anglesey town, Lanerchy*medd*, is probably

reminiscent of this famous mead. It is said that this town was also, or originally, Tafarn-y-medd, meaning *Mead Tavern*. (*The Welsh Bee Journal*, Vol. 2, No. 11, p. 131.)

86. *The Mabinogion, op. cit.*, p. 278.
87. C. Squire, *Celtic Myth and Legend*, p. 346.
88. Standish O'Grady, *Silva Gadelica*, p. 221.
89. Eugene O'Curry, *Manners and Customs of the Ancient Irish*, Vol. I, p. ccclxxvii.
90. H. M. Ransome, *op. cit.*, p. 213.
91. Mayo's translation of *Ancient Irish Poetry*, p. 48.
92. *Old Celtic Romances*, p. 24.
93. László Zuckermann, " Bee Culture in Hungary ", *The Bee World*, Vol. IX, p. 55.
94. Hilda M. Ransome, *op. cit.*, p. 151.
95. Monica M. Gardner, *Poland*, 1942, p. 10.
96. Beck & Smedley, *op. cit.*, p. 163.
97. Latham, *Nationalities of Europe*, Vol. I, London, 1863, p. 24.
98. Latham, *op. cit.*, p. 23.
99. Hilda M. Ransome, *op. cit.*, p. 157.
100. *Kalevala*, Runo XX, Kirkby's transl.
101. Hilda M. Ransome, *op. cit.*, p. 178, quoting Abercromby, *Pre- and Proto-Finns*, Vol. II, p. 330.
102. Hilda M. Ransome, *op. cit.*, p. 292.
103. E. E. Evans-Pritchard, " Some Collective Expressions of Obscenity in Africa ", *JRAI* (*Journal of the Royal Anthropological Institute*), Vol. LIX, 1929, p. 319.
104. J. B. Griffiths, " Glimpses of a Nyika Tribe " (Waduruma), *JRAI*, Vol. LXV, 1935, p. 275.
105. A. L. Bennett, " Ethnographical Notes on the Fang ", *JRAI*, Vol. II, 1899, p. 82 ; J. van Wing, " Bakongo Incantations and prayers ", *JRAI*, Vol. LX, 1930, pp. 406, 409.
106. C. W. Hobley, " Further Researches into Kikuyu and Kamba Religious Beliefs and Customs ", *JRAI*, Vol. XLI, 1911, pp. 421, 442, and 445.
107. G. W. Huntingford, " Modern Hunters : Some Account of the Kâmelīlo-Kâpchepkendi Dorōbo (Okiek) of Kenya Colony ", *JRAI*, Vol. LIX, 1929, pp. 342, 345.
108. F. H. Melland, *In Witch-bound Africa*, 1923, p. 123.
109. D. Storrs Fox, " Further Notes on the Masai of Kenya Colony ", *JRAI*, Vol. LX, 1930, p. 452.
110. C. W. Hobley, *op. cit.*, pp. 444–445. The author uses the word *beer*, not ale.
111. Sir James Frazer, *Totemism and Exogamy*, Vol. II, p. 411.

I am indebted to Mr. Maurice Gregory of Redruth, Cornwall, for writing and giving me the recipe employed by the Abyssinians in making their mead-beer, which bears out this point that the liquor is drunk in the early stages while actively fermenting.

He writes that this liquor among the Abyssinians " is a national beverage and known by them as ' Tej ' (pronounced Tedge).

" 1 part of honey is mixed with 5 parts water and a handful of a herb called Geisha is added. The whole well mixed and put into an unglazed earthenware jar and exposed to the sun —the opening is covered—for 5 days by which time it is fully fermented. The result is a wholesome and refreshing beverage if not taken too liberally.

" The Geisha leaves give the liquor a slightly bitter taste, not unpleasant, and they accelerate fermentation.

" I have travelled a good deal throughout Abyssinia and can testify to the excellence of the product when made under hygienic conditions though I fear this is not always the case when found in the ' bush '."

112. C. W. Hobley, *Bantu Beliefs and Magic*, 1932, pp. 251–252.

113. Hilda M. Ransome, *op. cit.*, p. 298, quoting S. Bragg, *JRAI*, Vol. XXXIV, p. 127.

114. D. Storrs Fox, *op. cit.*

115. Hilda M. Ransome, *op. cit.*, p. 296, quoting Henri H. Junod, *Life of a South African Tribe*, London, 1912, Vol. I, p. 239.

116. *Encyclopaedia Britannica*, 14th edition, Vol. 18, p. 762, article "pulque "; E. B. Taylor, *Anthropology*, 1881, p. 268.

117. Sir Everard Im Thurn, *Thoughts, Talks and Tramps*, edited by R. R. Marett, Oxford, 1934, pp. 84–85.

118. Hilda M. Ransome, *op. cit.*, pp. 268–269, quoting Dr. Seler, *Mexican Chronology*, p. 49.

119. Hilda M. Ransome, *op. cit.*, p. 269, quoting D. G. Brinton, *American Hero Myths*, p. 156.

120. Hilda M. Ransome, *op. cit.*, p. 269.

121. P. Morton Shand, *A Book of Other Wines*, London, 1929, p. 145.

122. *Encyclopaedia Britannica*, 14th edition, Vol. 16, p. 811.

123. E. W. Lane, *An Account of the Manners and Customs of the Modern Egyptians*, 1890, pp. 303 ff.

124. Ge-bēorscype or ge-bēorscipe.

125. Our word *supper* is from the Anglo-Saxon *supan*, to drink. *Dinner*, in contrast, is from *dynan*, to feed. Therefore our own evening meal definitely refers to a drinking-time when ale, mead and wine were drunk. Again, evening, *aefen*, is " drinking time ", in contrast to morning, which is " hunting time ". D. H. Haig, " Yorkshire Dials ", *Yorkshire Archaeological Journal*, Vol. V, 1879, p. 172.

126. Þurh gebeorscypas = in companies, *per convivia*. See *The Gospel of St. Luke in Anglo-Saxon*, by James W. Bright, Oxford, 1893.

127. *Sikaru* was a powerful date-honey wine of the Babylonians. Presumably it was related to *Shakar*.

128. Pliny, XIV, 22.

129. *Widsith, Beowulf,* etc., *op. cit.,* lines 117, 480, 482, 493, 616–619, 1094, 1240, 2041.
130. F. W. Hackwood, *op. cit.,* p. 43.
131. *Encyclopaedia Britannica,* 14th edition, Vol. III, p. 314.
132. Owing to the failure to realize the fundamental distinction between ale and beer we now have complete confusion in the use of the words. As pointed out by E. Spencer, *The Flowing Bowl,* London, 1903, p. 50 : " In the Eastern counties of England, and over the great part of the kingdom, ale signifies strong, and beer small, malt liquor, but in the West these names mean exactly the reverse."
133. Chaucer, *Monk's Prologue,* lines B. 3081–3084.
134. Hieronymus Cardanus (Jerome Cardan) (1552). *De rerum varietate.* Paris, 1643, taken from a summary in *P.S.A.S.,* Vol. XI, Third Series, p. 459.
135. W. W. Skeat, *Chaucer,* Oxford, 1904, p. 177.
136. Judges, 13, 5, 7 : *Chaucer,* B. 3245.
137. W. Cambden, *Britannia,* 1789, Vol. III, p. 752, where it states the *sisere* was made from pears.
138. F. W. Hackwood, *op. cit.,* p. 41.
139. At the house of Mr. Lewis Parry, at Halesworth, Suffolk, on whom I was billeted in 1940–41 when Battery Captain in the 222 Anti-Tank Battery R.A.
140. C. W. Radcliffe Cooke, *A Book about Cider and Perry,* London, 1898, p. 3.
141. C. W. Radcliffe, *ut supra.*
142. Isaac Taylor, *Words and Places,* London, 1865, p. 260.
143. Pecock, *Repr.,* 1, XX, 121, 1449.
144. F. W. Hackwood, *op. cit.,* p. 331.
145. Hilda M. Ransome, *op. cit.,* p. 142.
146. Chaucer, lines A. 2275–2280.
147. Chaucer, lines B. 2035–2046.
148. Chaucer, lines 3371–3382.
149. Towneley, *Myst.,* xxviii, 111.
150. W. Shakespeare, *Love's Labour Lost,* Act V, Sc. II ; and *The Merry Wives of Windsor,* Act V, line 167.
151. Welsh scholars say that it does not mean a " spiced mead " but a " spiced drink or wine " the *medd* being purely fortuitous, although, of course, it is always used for a spiced mead. *Meddyg* is related to the Latin *medicus,* meaning healing or medicinal, and *llyn* is liquor, being the root of this word.
152. Elyot, *Castle of Helthe,* 1541.
153. Rowley, *Match at Midnight,* II, i, 1633.
154. Butler, *Fem. Mon.,* XX, ii, 1623.
155. Venner, *Via Recta,* ii, 41, 1620.
156. Samuel Pepys, *Diary,* 25th July, 1666.
157. B. Googe, *Heresbach's Husb.,* II (1586), 586.

158. *The Coverley Papers from " The Spectator "*, edited by O. M. Myers, Oxford Press, 1927, pp. 131–132, from *Spectator* of Tuesday, May 20.

159. Mrs. Delany, *Life and Correspondence*, II, 463 (1861).

160. Tobias Smollett, *Humphry Clinker*, Oxford Press, 1925, p. 403.

161. Robert Southey, *Madoc*, stanza 4, pt. II.

162. How much mead passed out of general knowledge by the nineteenth century is illustrated by the following, from an American work, which probably represents a high-water mark in ignorance connected with this subject. *The Century Dictionary* (1890) says—" a sweet drink charged with carbonic gas, and flavoured with some syrup, as sarsaparilla ! "

163. Thorold Rogers, *History of Agriculture and Prices in England*, Vol. I, p. 418 ; V, p. 327 ; VI, p. 237.

164. *Encyclopaedia Britannica*, 14th edition, Vol. 23, p. 686.

165. *Encyclopaedia Britannica*, 14th edition, Vol. I, p. 553.

166. Hilda M. Ransome, *op. cit.*, pp. 146–147.

167. Thus, to cite only a few such allusions : Milton's *History of Muscovy* (1674), " Their drink is better, being sundry sorts of meath " ; Burton's *Anatomy of Melancholy* (1621), " Be merry together . . . as our modern Muscovites do in their Mede-inns " ; *Spectacle de la Nature* (1757), Vol II., p. 256 (eighth edition), " The Lithuanians, the Poles, and the Muscovites, who have plenty of honey, steep it in water, which they boil to a moderate degree, and then suffer the Mixture to ferment in the Sun, by which Means it becomes a very strong and pleasing Liquor, and is commonly known by the Name of Mead."

168. *A New System of Domestic Cookery*, by a Lady, London, 1827, p. 347.

169. *The Closet of the Eminently Learned Sir Kenelme Digbie Kt. opened : London, 1669*, and the same re-printed by Philip Lee Warner, London, 1910, and edited by Anne MacDonell.

170. Isaac Taylor, *Words and Places*, London, 1865, p. 291.

171. T. G. Shaw, *Wine, the Vine, and the Cellar*, London, 1864, pp. 449–450.

172. T. G. Shaw, *op. cit.*, pp. 229–230.

173. Chaucer, *The Pardoner's Tale*, lines 562–571.

174. Dionisius Petavius, *A Geographical Description of the World*, London, 1659, p. 118.

175. F. W. Hackwood, *op. cit.*, p. 330.

176. W. Shakespeare, *The Merry Wives of Windsor*, Act V, line 167.

177. Varro, III, 15.

178. Columella, XII, 41.

179. Virgil, *Georgics*, IV, 101–102.

180. Tickner Edwardes, *The Lore of the Honey-Bee*, London, 1912, p. 31.

181. Pliny, 51–53.

182. Plutarch, *Theseus*, 22.
183. *The Goodman of Paris*, translated by Eileen Power, London, 1928, p. 238.
184. Rabelais, Bk. III, cap. XXXII.
185. Sharon Turner, *op. cit.*, Vol. III, p. 36.
186. T. G. Shaw, *op. cit.*, pp. 271, 276, 277.
187. Warner's *Antiquitates Culinaviae*, 1791, p. 90.
188. Maurice Healy, *Stay me with Flagons*, London, 1940, p. 108. I do not think, incidentally, that his recipe is the best that could be found for making pyment.
189. F. W. Hackwood, *op. cit.*, p. 321.
190. Edward Spencer, *The Flowing Bowl*, 1903, pp. 32–33.
191. Edward Spencer, *op. cit.*, pp. 28–29.
192. Dionisius Petavius, *op. cit.*, p. 321.
193. Dorothy Hartley and Margaret M. Elliott, *Life and Work of the People of England : The Seventeenth Century*, London, p. 32. Later variants of this Birch wine substituted sugar, to the detriment of the liquor no doubt, for honey. Edward Spencer gives the following recipe and account of this unusual drink : " In March the ends of the birch boughs are cut off, and bottles are suspended from them. To every gallon of liquor add 1 lb. sugar. Yeast is added and fermented : mace and cinnamon added. Said to be ' a most delicate, brisk wine, of a flavour like unto Rhenish '." (*The Flowing Bowl*, London, 1903, pp. 30–31.) He also recounts the alleged virtues of this wine against " the stone " and as a " powerful curer of the Ptisick ".
194. Strabo, Book IV, 5.
195. Beck & Smedley, *op. cit.*, p. 90, state *brag* means malt and *got* honeycomb.
196. Mabinogion, *op. cit.*, p. 114.
197. Hilda M. Ransome, *op. cit.*, p. 142.
198. *The Goodman of Paris*, *op. cit.*, pp. 293–294.
199. *Encyclopaedia Britannica*, 13th edition, Vol. 13, p. 654.
200. *Encyclopaedia Britannica*, 14th edition, Vol. 21, article on " Spirits ", p. 241, quoting Fairley, *The Analyst*, 1905.
201. *A Plain Plantain*, arranged by R. G. Alexander, Ditchling, Sussex, 1922, pp. 2–4.
202. Edward Spencer, *op. cit.*, pp. 27–28.
203. Edward Spencer, *op. cit.*, p. 30.
     Not all the recipes, however, were as degenerate as these. A notable exception for its avoidance of spices and unnecessary flavourings is that contained in *The True Amazons : or, the Monarchy of Bees* by Joseph Warder of Croydon, Physician (1765), where we read :
     " One hundred and twenty pounds will make a Barrel of very good Mead : But if you make it of clear Honey, then your best way is to allow four pounds to every gallon of

Water. Let your Quantity be much or little, (which you ought to govern yourself by either considering the Bigness of your Cask, or the Quantity of Honey you have to make up into Mead) mix it in your Copper, and then boil it, and scum it well ; . . . when your Mead is almost cold, tun it up, clay it down, and let it stand till it is fine, and old enough to drink ; which sometimes will be sooner than other, according to the Time of the Year and the weather that comes upon it after making. This Liquor is one of the choicest of Wines, as well as the most wholesome of all Vinous Liquors in the World, and ought to be drank and made use of in Possets, &c. as *Canary* ; and thus used, it is impossible to know whether the Posset was made of your Mead or Canary "

204. *A New System of Domestic Cookery*, by a Lady, London, 1827.

205. Mary Woodman, *Home-made Wines*, London, p. 34.

206. Dr. Druit, *Report on Cheap Wine*, London, 1865, p. 130.

207. Druit, *op. cit.*, pp. 127–128.

208. Druit, *op. cit.*, p. 128.

209. Druit, *op. cit.*, p. 128.

210. Druit, *op. cit.*, p. 127.

211. That is why, no doubt, honey can be taken successfully in certain cases of diabetes. I have known at least one case that has alleged its cure was due to a diet of honey.

212. E. F. Phillips, " Honey as a Food ", *The Bee World*, Vol. XI, p. 36.

213. E. B. Wedmore, *A Manual of Beekeeping*, London, 1946, p. 107.

214. Leonard S. Harker, " Honey and Vitamins ", *The Bee World*, Vol. X, pp. 119–120. Beck & Smedley, *op. cit.*, pp. 35–36, 38.

215. E. B. Wedmore, *op. cit.*

216. Tickner Edwardes, *The Lore of the Honey-Bee*, London, 1912, p. 181.

217. Captain Egon Rotter, " Honey : Its Origin, Appearance, Use ", etc., *The Bee World*, Vol. X, pp. 88–89.

218. Egon Rotter, *ut supra*.

219. Egon Rotter, *ut supra*.

220. See Lord Cherwell, " Is Britain Worse Fed than in War Time ? ", *Daily Telegraph and Morning Post*, Thursday, 6th February, 1947, for calories in the British diet. According to Beck & Smedley, *op. cit.*, p. 45, the calories in honey are as high as 1600.

221. E. F. Phillips, *op. cit.*

222. Egon Rotter, *op. cit.*

223. Beck & Smedley, *op. cit.*, pp. 94–95. It might be added that Dioscorides, a first-century Greek physician, whose *Materia Medica* is one of the oldest, praised the healing properties of mead.

224. Referred to by P. Morton Shand, *A Book of Other Wines*, London, 1929, p. 131.

225. Charles Tovey, *Wine and Wine Countries*, London, 1877.
226. Julius Caesar, *De Bello Gallico*, VI, cap. XXVI.
227. *Mabinogion, op. cit.*, p. 378, note on p. 152.
228. *Heimskringla, op. cit.*, p. 60. XV.
229. *Heimskringla, op. cit.*, p. 244, XI, 3.
230. William Cambden, *op. cit.*, Vol. 3, p. 531, Plate XLIV.
231. E. P. How, *Proceedings of the Society of Antiquaries of Scotland* (*PSAS*), 1933–34, Vol. LXVIII, 6th Series, Vol. 8, p. 394.
232. *Archaeological Journal*, London, 1846, Vol. III, p. 361.
233. Rabelais, Book I, cap. XXXIX.
234. F. W. Hackwood, *op. cit.*, p. 320.
235. Theocritus, *op. cit., Thyrsis*, 29.
236. *Heimskringla, op. cit.*, p. 179.
237. *Heimskringla, op. cit.*, p. 243.
238. *Heimskringla, op. cit.*, p. 35.
239. *Heimskringla, op. cit.*, p. 334.
240. Sharon Turner, *op. cit.*, Vol. III, p. 61.
241. Sharon Turner, *ut supra*.
242. *Widsith, Beowulf*, etc., *op. cit.*, p. 76, lines 2253–2254 ; p. 77, line 2282.
243. J. H. Stevenson, " The Bannatyne or Bute Mazer ", *PSAS*, 1930–31, LXV, 6th Series, Vol. 5, pp. 226–227.
244. J. H. Stevenson, *ut supra*.
245. Sir Charles Jackson, *Illustrated History of English Plate*.
246. *The Yorkshire Archaeological Journal*, Vol. VIII, 1884, pp. 311–312.
247. E. P. How, *op. cit.*, p. 395.
248. *The Yorkshire Archaeological Journal, op. cit.*, p. 403.
249. *Rites of Durham, Surtees Society*, Vol. XV, pp. 68–69.
250. *Testamenta Karlaolensia, The Series of Wills from Prae-Reformation Registers of the Bishops of Carlisle*, 1353–86, edited by R. S. Ferguson, *Cumberland and Westmoreland Archaeological Society*, 1893, pp. 54, 3, 16, 17, 73.
251. Percy's *Reliques*, 4th edition, Vol. III, p. 94.
252. Edm. Spenser, *Shepherd's Calendar, August*.
253. F. W. Hackwood, *op. cit.*, pp. 330–331.
254. W. J. Cripps, *Old English Plate*, London, 1905, p. 286.
255. Rev. Thomas Burns, *Old Scottish Communion Plate*.
256. E. P. How, *op. cit.*, pp. 396, 398, 400, 408.
257. I have several modern ones.
258. Chaucer, B. 2041–2042.
259. G. Clinch, *Handbook of English Antiquities*, 1905, p. 321.
260. Rabelais, Book V, cap. X.
261. W. McGill, B.A., *Old Ross-Shire and Scotland*, Vol. II, p. 30, Doc. No. 1061, dated 1722.
262. It is said that Professor Zander has proved that the honey varies with the type of bee. Capt. Egon Rotter, *op. cit.*
263. Tickner Edwardes, *op. cit.*, p. 19.

264. Rev. R. Valpy French, *The History of Toasting*, London, 1881, pp. 29–30.
265. Rev. R. Valpy French, *op. cit.*, p. 34.
266. Washington Irving, *Old Christmas*, London, 1903, p. 164.
267. Rev. R. Valpy French, *op. cit.*, p. 32.
268. Rev. R. Valpy French, *op. cit.*, p. 35.
269. T. G. Shaw, *op. cit.*, pp. 272–273.

MEAD

BOOKS for Brewers and Beer Lovers

Order Now ... Your Brew Will Thank You!

These books offered by Brewers Publications are some of the most sought-after reference tools for homebrewers and professional brewers alike. Filled with tips, techniques, recipes and history, these books will help you expand your brewing horizons. Let the world's foremost brewers help you as you brew. Whatever your brewing level or interest, Brewers Publications has the information necessary for you to brew the best beer in the world — your beer.

MEAD

BREWERS PUBLICATIONS ORDER FORM

PROFESSIONAL BREWING BOOKS

QTY.	TITLE	STOCK #	PRICE	EXT. PRICE
_____	Brewery Planner	500	80.00	_____
_____	North American Brewers Resource Directory	505	80.00	_____
_____	Principles of Brewing Science	463	29.95	_____

THE BREWERY OPERATIONS SERIES
from Micro- and Pubbrewers Conferences

QTY.	TITLE	STOCK #	PRICE	EXT. PRICE
_____	Volume 6, 1989 Conference	536	25.95	_____
_____	Volume 7, 1990 Conference	537	25.95	_____
_____	Volume 8, 1991 Conference, Brewing Under Adversity	538	25.95	_____
_____	Volume 9, 1992 Conference, Quality Brewing — Share the Experience	539	25.95	_____

CLASSIC BEER STYLE SERIES

QTY.	TITLE	STOCK #	PRICE	EXT. PRICE
_____	Pale Ale	401	11.95	_____
_____	Continental Pilsener	402	11.95	_____
_____	Lambic	403	11.95	_____
_____	Vienna, Märzen, Oktoberfest	404	11.95	_____
_____	Porter	405	11.95	_____
_____	Belgian Ale	406	11.95	_____
_____	German Wheat Beer	407	11.95	_____
_____	Scotch Ale	408	11.95	_____
_____	Bock	409	11.95	_____

BEER AND BREWING SERIES, for homebrewers and beer enthusiasts, from National Homebrewers Conference

QTY.	TITLE	STOCK #	PRICE	EXT. PRICE
_____	Volume 8, 1988 Conference	448	21.95	_____
_____	Volume 10, 1990 Conference	450	21.95	_____
_____	Volume 11, 1991 Conference, Brew Free or Die!	451	21.95	_____
_____	Volume 12, 1992 Conference, Just Brew It!	452	21.95	_____

GENERAL BEER AND BREWING INFORMATION

QTY.	TITLE	STOCK #	PRICE	EXT. PRICE
_____	The Art of Cidermaking	468	9.95	_____
_____	Brewing Lager Beer	460	14.95	_____
_____	Brewing Mead	461	11.95	_____
_____	Dictionary of Beer and Brewing	462	19.95	_____
_____	Evaluating Beer	465	19.95	_____
_____	Great American Beer Cookbook	466	24.95	_____
_____	Victory Beer Recipes	467	11.95	_____
_____	Winners Circle	464	11.95	_____

SUBTOTAL _____

Call or write for a free Beer Enthusiast catalog today.
• U.S. funds only.
• All Brewers Publications books come with a money-back guarantee.
* **Postage & Handling:** $4 for the first book ordered, plus $1 for each book thereafter. For Canadian and international orders please add $5 for the first book and $2 for each book thereafter. Orders cannot be shipped without appropriate P&H.

Colo. Residents Add 3% Sales Tax _____

P&H *_____

TOTAL _____

Brewers Publications, PO Box 1510, Boulder, CO 80306-1510, USA;
(303) 546-6514; Internet orders@aob.org; FAX (303) 447-2825.

MEAD